Creating your MySQL Database: Practical Design Tips and Techniques

A short guide for everyone on how to structure their data and set up their MySQL database tables efficiently and easily

Marc Delisle

BIRMINGHAM - MUMBAI

Creating your MySQL Database: Practical Design Tips and Techniques

First published: November 2006

Production Reference: 1141106

Published by Packt Publishing Ltd.
32 Lincoln Road
Olton
Birmingham, B27 6PA, UK.

ISBN 1-904811-30-2

www.packtpub.com

Cover Image by www.visionwt.com

Credits

Author

Marc Delisle

Reviewer

Rudy Limeback

Development Editor

Louay Fatoohi

Assistant Development Editor

Nikhil Bangera

Technical Editor

Mithil Kulkarni

Editorial Manager

Dipali Chittar

Project Manager

Patricia Weir

Indexer

Bhushan Pangaonkar

Proofreader

Martin Brooks

Layouts and Illustrations

Shantanu Zagade

Cover Designer

Shantanu Zagade

About the Author

Marc Delisle is a member of the MySQL Developers Guild, which regroups community developers — because of his involvement with phpMyAdmin. He started to contribute to this popular MySQL web interface in December 1998, when he made the first multi-language version. He has been actively involved with the phpMyAdmin project since May 2001 as a developer and project administrator.

He has worked since 1980 at Collège de Sherbrooke, Québec, Canada, as an application programmer and network manager. He has also been teaching networking, security, Linux servers, and PHP/MySQL application development.

I would like to thank the whole Packt team for their support, especially Louay Fatoohi and Nikhil Bangera; their advice helped shaping this book. My thanks also go to Rudy Limeback for his insight.

The developers of the MySQL software have earned my respect; may they find here my warm gratitude for their excellent product.

I hope that this book will assist readers into building effective data structures.

To Carole, André, Corinne, Annie, and Guillaume, with all my love.

About the Reviewer

Rudy Limeback is an SQL Consultant with close to 20 years of experience using SQL in one database system or another. He is located in Toronto, Canada but, thanks to the miracle that is the Internet, consults for clients all over the wide world. More information on SQL and Web development can be found on Rudy's website, `http://www.r937.com/`.

Table of Contents

Preface

MySQL, launched in 1995, has become the most popular open source database system. The popularity of MySQL and phpMyAdmin has allowed many non-IT specialists to build dynamic websites with a MySQL backend. This book is a short but complete guide showing beginners how to design good data structures for MySQL. It teaches how to plan the data structure and how to implement it physically using MySQL's model.

What This Book Covers

Chapter 1 introduces the concept of MySQL, and discusses MySQL's growing popularity and its impact as a powerful tool. This chapter gives us a brief overview of the relational models and Codd's rules, which are required for designing purposes. A brief introduction to our case study — "car dealer" is provided at the end.

Chapter 2 shows how to deal with the raw data information that comes from the users or other sources, and the techniques that can help us build a comprehensive data collection. Also, this chapter covers the exact limits of the analyzed system, how one should gather documents, and interview activities for our case study.

Chapter 3 emphasises on transforming the data elements gathered in the collection process into a cohesive set of column names. The concept of data naming is also discussed in this chapter.

Chapter 4 provides the technique of grouping column names into tables. Rules for table layout, the concepts such as primary key, unique key, data redundancy, and data dependency are covered in this chapter.

Chapter 5 presents various techniques for improving our data structure in terms of security, performance, and documentation. The final data structure for the car dealer's case study is provided at the end.

Chapter 6 covers a supplemental case study about an airline system. This case study involves various steps such as gathering documents, preparing preliminary list of data elements, preparing a list of tables, sample values, and queries for the airline system.

What You Need for This Book

Basic knowledge of SQL is required. Emphasis is made on the phpMyAdmin web-based interface for reproducing the examples, although the "mysql" command-line tool can be used. No knowledge of MySQL server administration or any specific operating system is required.

Conventions

In this book, you will find a number of styles of text that distinguish between different kinds of information. Here are some examples of these styles, and an explanation of their meaning.

There are three styles for code. Code words in text are shown as follows: "In this case, we can add employee information, the employee code to the car_event table".

A block of code will be set as follows:

```
CREATE TABLE `event` (
  `code` int(11) NOT NULL,
  `description` char(40) NOT NULL,
  PRIMARY KEY  (`code`)
) ENGINE=MyISAM DEFAULT CHARSET=latin1;

INSERT INTO `event` VALUES (1, 'washed');
```

When we wish to draw your attention to a particular part of a code block, the relevant lines or items will be made bold:

```
CREATE TABLE `event` (
  `code` int(11) NOT NULL,
  `description` char(40) NOT NULL,
  PRIMARY KEY  (`code`)
) ENGINE=MyISAM DEFAULT CHARSET=latin1;

INSERT INTO `event` VALUES (1, 'washed');
```

New terms and **important words** are introduced in a bold-type font. Words that you see on the screen, in menus, or dialog boxes for example, appear in our text like this: "It becomes impossible to link this "column" (for example the **special paint color**) to a lookup table".

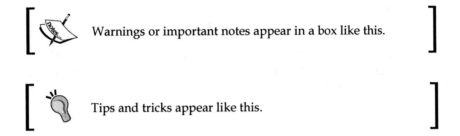

Warnings or important notes appear in a box like this.

Tips and tricks appear like this.

Reader Feedback

Feedback from our readers is always welcome. Let us know what you think about this book, what you liked or may have disliked. Reader feedback is important for us to develop titles that you really get the most out of.

To send us general feedback, simply drop an email to feedback@packtpub.com, making sure to mention the book title in the subject of your message.

If there is a book that you need and would like to see us publish, please send us a note in the **SUGGEST A TITLE** form on www.packtpub.com or email suggest@packtpub.com.

If there is a topic that you have expertise in and you are interested in either writing or contributing to a book, see our author guide on www.packtpub.com/authors.

Customer Support

Now that you are the proud owner of a Packt book, we have a number of things to help you to get the most from your purchase.

Downloading the Example Code for the Book

Visit http://www.packtpub.com/support, and select this book from the list of titles to download any example code or extra resources for this book. The files available for download will then be displayed.

The downloadable files contain instructions on how to use them.

Errata

Although we have taken every care to ensure the accuracy of our contents, mistakes do happen. If you find a mistake in one of our books—maybe a mistake in text or code—we would be grateful if you would report this to us. By doing this you can save other readers from frustration, and help to improve subsequent versions of this book. If you find any errata, report them by visiting http://www.packtpub.com/ support, selecting your book, clicking on the **Submit Errata** link, and entering the details of your errata. Once your errata have been verified, your submission will be accepted and the errata added to the list of existing errata. The existing errata can be viewed by selecting your title from http://www.packtpub.com/support.

Questions

You can contact us at questions@packtpub.com if you are having a problem with some aspect of the book, and we will do our best to address it.

1
Introducing MySQL Design

Data design is an essential part of the application development cycle. By analogy, building an application is like building a house. Having the right tools is important, but we need a solid foundation: the data structure. However, producing a good data structure can be a daunting challenge; the quest for a perfect data structure can lead us to new territories where many methods are available. Which one is the best? How can we keep our focus on the goal to achieve, without losing our time?

Data design for MySQL databases is both a science and an art, and there must be a good balance between the scientific and the empiric aspects of the method. The scientific aspect refers to information technology (IT) principles, whereas the empiric facet is mostly based on intuitions and experience.

This book is primarily oriented towards MySQL databases. It teaches how to plan the data structure and how to implement it physically using MySQL's model. The planning part is sometimes referred to as *logical design*, but it is preferable to view the logical/physical process as a whole.

MySQL's Popularity and Impact

MySQL (www.mysql.com), launched in 1995, has become the most popular open source database system. Virtually all web providers include MySQL as part of their hosting plan, often on the ubiquitous LAMP (Linux, Apache, MySQL, PHP) platform. Another root cause of MySQL's popularity has been the ongoing success of phpMyAdmin (www.phpmyadmin.net), a well-established MySQL web-based interface. Therefore many websites use MySQL as their back-end data repository.

The Need for MySQL Design

Overall, MySQL's popularity has attracted many web developers, some of them having no prior IT experience. When faced with the task of transforming a static website into a dynamic/transactional one, or integrating corporate data into the site, developers are sometimes inclined to improvise a data structure. This structure (or lack of structure) may work for a certain time but later fails because of lack of depth. Maybe the system initially works because it started small, with only a few functions planned and implemented, but falls apart when users ask more of it. A poorly designed data structure can only be patched to a certain extent. It can also have scaling issues, when the initial testing has been done with only a few rows of data.

The apparent facility of using the tools may hide the fact that database design depends upon essential principles. Eluding them can render an application costly to maintain, because correcting data structural errors after application coding has begun is time consuming.

"What do I do Next?"

Here is an example of the impact of MySQL in the ranks of non-IT people. I once saw this question in a phpMyAdmin discussion forum – I am citing it from memory: "I've installed MySQL and phpMyAdmin, now I need directions: what do I do next?" I answered "Maybe you could create a table, and then insert some data into it. Next you could browse for your data."

Clearly, those tools were perceived as interesting by this person, but I can only wonder what kind of table structure came into existence after this forum conversation.

Data Design Steps

We can think of data design as a sequence of steps whose goal is to produce the physical MySQL databases, tables, and columns necessary to support an application.

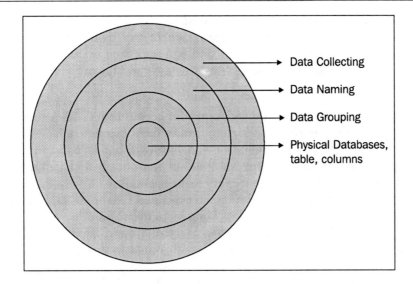

Starting with the outer shell, we first need to learn about our data by collecting it. We then start to organize these data elements by naming them appropriately. This is followed by regrouping the data elements into tables, taking into account the needed keys. Whereas the previous steps could have been done only on paper, the final step is to implement the model within MySQL's structure.

All these steps are covered in distinct chapters of this book.

Data as a Resource

Before examining the various techniques available for design, let's think about the concept of data itself.

Organizations and enterprises use many assets, for example buildings, furniture, brains, but perhaps the most valuable asset is information or data. We remark that data documents the enterprise's procedures, and binds people into an ongoing exchange of information, called information flow. Computers help to formalize this data but we have to remember that it exists by itself.

But this is my Data!

When building data designs, we have to meet users and understand the enterprise's data flow. In an ideal world, every department, including the IT department, and every user would collaborate in order to help data flow easily between departments. However, from time to time, one can witness two attitudes that impede the normal data flow in enterprises. The first one is that some IT departments, having the responsibility for the computers where data resides, come to think that the data is theirs. This has the effect of keeping a certain level of secrecy that hides data and can block the data design process. The second one is a variation of the first one, this time caused by a user – data originates from this user and he has a tendency not to share it.

As an example of this latter attitude, let's consider accounting data. Before the PC era, accounting systems existed inside mainframes or minicomputers, and the IT department managed all data including accounting data. Since the advent of microcomputers and spreadsheet applications, an accounting clerk can manage a great deal of data, producing high-quality reports about it. However, this data often resides on his computer; he enters it, he produces the report, and he gets the accolades for it from his boss. So the data belongs to the accounting clerk, right? This way of thinking impedes data flow between individuals and departments and has a tendency of leading to redundant, disjoint data throughout the organization.

After the data design process, bridges are built between these isolated data islands created by users or departments so that the data can benefit the whole enterprise. It may also happen that fewer islands exist and redundant data is eliminated.

Data Modeling

Data is normally organized into an information system. This system can be compared to something as simple as a loose-sheet binder, however this book describes the data design process in the context of computer-based information systems, or databases. Moreover, databases follow a design model, and we will use the most popular one – the **relational model**.

The complete data collection of an enterprise is larger than what our model will encompass.

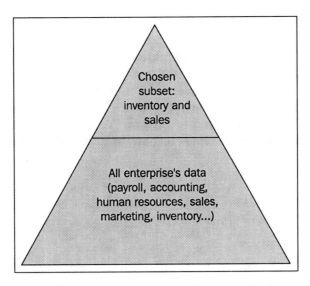

We will build a model that represents only a subset of the data spectrum. The question is which subset? We'll see in Chapter 2 that we must set boundaries to the analyzed system's data scope.

To build information systems that last, data must be tamed and molded to correctly represent reality. *Correctly* here means:

- Follow the needs of the organization, including the system's boundaries
- Conform to the chosen data design model (here, the relational one)
- Possess a high degree of adaptability to adjust itself to the changing environment

Overview of the Relational Model

We owe to Dr. Edgar F. Codd the concept of the relational model, from his 1970 paper *A Relational Model of Data for Large Shared Data Banks* (http://www.acm.org/classics/nov95/toc.html). Dr. Codd later explained his model by defining a set of rules – the so-called Codd's Twelve rules (http://en.wikipedia.org/wiki/Codd%27s_12_rules). An ideal database management system (DBMS) would implement all those rules, but few if any do. But this is not a problem in practice since the benefits of the relational model are achieved even in products that do not apply all the rules. We are perfectly capable of building an efficient relational data design with currently available database products like MySQL.

When dealing with data design, I believe that the most important rules are number 1 and number 2. Here is a summary of these two Codd's rules.

Rule #1

This rule states that data is contained in **tables**. A table logically regroups information about a certain subject, for example, cars. The tabular format – rows and columns is the important idea here. A row describes information about a single item, for example, a specific car, whereas a column describes a single characteristic (or attribute) of each item, for example, its color. We will see in Chapter 3 that the decomposition of data into well-adjusted columns is important to have a flexible and useful structure.

The intersection of a row and a column contains the value of a specific attribute for a single item. We sometimes refer to this intersection as a cell containing our data – this is the same idea as in a spreadsheet.

Rule #2

Data is not retrieved or referenced by physical location – *find the third record in this file*. Instead, data must be fetched by referencing a table, a unique key – the **primary key** – and one or many column names. For example, with the cars table, we use the car serial number to retrieve this car's color.

This rule will be studied in Chapter 4, where we describe data grouping and the concept of choosing keys. Proper key choosing is of utmost importance.

Simplified Design Technique

Many years ago, I started to elaborate data structures using the relational model. I was using a method that could be summarized by this sentence: "determine where the data fits the best in the structure". Then I learned about the design techniques that were taught to IT specialists and evolved from the relational model.

The technique, which is frequently taught consists of building an **entity-relationship diagram**. In this kind of diagram, we represent nouns, for example, a car, a customer, using entities, and the relationships between them are expressed using verbs. An example of relationship binding two entities is "a customer buys a car". When the diagram is done, it must be somewhat transformed into a model consisting of tables and columns, using a technique called **normalization** that uses many steps to refine the model into an effective data structure.

These techniques produce reports, diagrams, and eventually a theoretical data design that can be implemented physically in a DBMS.

When I became familiar with those traditional techniques, I thought that for me at least they were a loss of time. Those methods teach a way but the ultimate goal – a working relational database and associated documentation can be achieved more directly. Moreover, those techniques suffer a problem: they cannot be applied blindfolded and mechanically. The developer always has to **think** about data naming, data grouping, and choosing keys while trying to balance users' needs and constraints imposed by:

- the hardware
- the chosen database management system
- planned growth
- time
- budget

I realized that the traditional techniques are taught everywhere, and I respect the teachers who teach them. But believe me, when it's time to deliver an application notwithstanding the interface itself, it's important to avoid losing time to intermediate by-products and go straightforward to a working prototype. Using a more direct method during the data design phase frees more time to refine the interface, to catch unforeseen needs and address them.

This book's goal is to teach the minimum principles one has to apply in order to build an effective data structure.

Case Study

The various steps of data design can be explained in a very practical way by using two case studies. A case study is the best way of explaining ideas that can somewhat become too abstract without real examples. Chapters 1 through 5 are based on a single case study: "Car dealership". Chapter 6 consists of another case study that recapitulates all the notions seen in the previous chapters.

Our Car Dealer

Suppose we've been contacted by a car dealer who wants to computerize parts of his business. Let's describe a little bit about this business. In Chapter 2, we will examine the data collecting phase for our system more formally.

This car dealer operates at a single address. They employ nine salespersons who dutifully welcome potential customers and show them the car models that are available on the floor. In addition, two store assistants handle car movements, and an office clerk takes notes about customers' appointments. Fontax and Licorne are the two fictitious brands offered by this dealer. Each brand has a number of models, for example Mitsou, Wanderer, and Gazelle.

The System's Goals

We want to keep information about the cars' inventory and sales. The following are some sample questions that demonstrate the kind of information our system will have to deal with:

- How many cars of Fontax Mitsou 2007 do we have in stock?
- How many visitors test-drove the Wanderer last year?
- How many Wanderer cars did we sell during a certain period?
- Who is our best salesperson for Mitsou, Wanderer, or overall in 2007?
- Are buyers mostly men or women (per car model)?

Here are the titles of some reports that are needed by this car dealer:

- Detailed sales per month: salesperson, number of cars, revenue
- Yearly sales per salesperson
- Inventory efficiency: average delay for car delivery to the dealer, or to the customer
- Visitors report: percentage of visitors trying a car; percentage of road tests that lead to a sale
- Customer satisfaction about the salesperson
- The sales contract

In addition to this, screen applications must be built to support the inventory and sales activities. For example, being able to consult and update the appointment schedule; consult the car delivery schedule for the next week.

After this data model is built, the remaining phases of the application development cycle, such as screen and report design, will provide this car dealer with reports, and on-line applications to manage the car inventory and the sales in a better way.

The Tale of the Too Wide Table

This book focuses on representing data in MySQL. The containers of tables in MySQL, and other products are the databases. It is quite possible to have just one table in a database and thus avoid fully applying the relational model concept in which tables are related to each other through common values; however we will use the model in its normal way: having many tables and creating relations between them.

This section describes an example of data crammed into one huge table, also called a *too wide table* because it is formed with too many columns. This *too wide table* is fundamentally *non-relational*.

Sometimes the data structure needs to be reviewed or evaluated, as it might be based on poor decisions in terms of data naming conventions, key choosing, and the number of tables. Probably the most common problem is that the whole data is put into one big, wide table.

The reason for this common structure (or lack of structure) is that many developers think in terms of the results or even of the printed results. Maybe they know how to build a spreadsheet and try to apply spreadsheet principles to databases. Let's assume that the main goal of building a database is to produce this sales report, which shows how many cars were sold in each month, by each salesperson, describing the brand name, the car model number, and the name.

Salesperson	Period	Brand Name	Car model number	Car model name and year	Quantity sold
Murray, Dan	2006-01	Fontax	1A8	Mitsou 2007	3
Murray, Dan	2006-01	Fontax	2X12	Wanderer 2006	7
Murray, Dan	2006-02	Fontax	1A8	Mitsou 2007	4
Smith, Peter	2006-01	Fontax	1A8	Mitsou 2007	1
Smith, Peter	2006-01	Licorne	LKC	Gazelle 2007	1
Smith, Peter	2006-02	Licorne	LKC	Gazelle 2007	6

Without thinking much about the implications of this structure, we could build just one table, `sales`:

salesperson	brand	model_number	model_name_year	qty_2006_01	qty_2006_02
Murray, Dan	Fontax	1A8	Mitsou 2007	3	4
Murray, Dan	Fontax	2X12	Wanderer 2006	7	
Smith, Peter	Fontax	1A8	Mitsou 2007	1	
Smith, Peter	Licorne	LKC	Gazelle 2007	1	6

At first sight, we have tabularized all the information that is needed for the report.

The book's examples can be reproduced using the `mysql` command-line utility, or phpMyAdmin, a more intuitive web interface. You can refer to *Mastering phpMyAdmin 2.8 for Effective MySQL Management* book from Packt Publishing (ISBN 1-904811-60-6). In phpMyAdmin, the exact commands may be typed in using the SQL Query Window, or we can benefit from the menus and graphical dialogs. Both ways will be shown throughout the book.

Here is the statement we would use to create the `sales` table with the `mysql` command-line utility:

```
CREATE TABLE sales (
    salesperson char(40) NOT NULL,
    brand char(40) NOT NULL,
    model_number char(40) NOT NULL,
    model_name_year char(40) NOT NULL,
    qty_2006_01 int(11) NOT NULL,
    qty_2006_02 int(11) NOT NULL
) ENGINE=MyISAM DEFAULT CHARSET=latin1;
```

In the previous statement, while `char(40)` means a column with 40 characters, `int(11)` means an integer with a display width of 11 in MySQL.

Using the phpMyAdmin web interface instead, we would obtain:

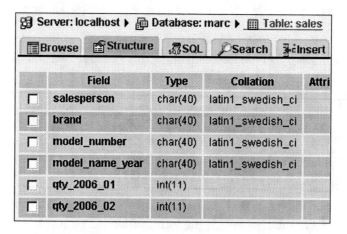

Here we have entered sample data into our `sales` table:

```
INSERT INTO sales VALUES ('Murray, Dan', 'Fontax', '1A8',
'Mitsou 2007', 3, 4);
INSERT INTO sales VALUES ('Murray, Dan', 'Fontax', '2X12',
'Wanderer 2006', 7, 0);
INSERT INTO sales VALUES ('Smith, Peter', 'Licorne', 'LKC',
'Gazelle 2007', 1, 6);
INSERT INTO sales VALUES ('Smith, Peter', 'Fontax', '1A8',
'Mitsou 2007', 1, 0);
```

←T→	salesperson	brand	model_number	model_name_year	qty_2006_01	qty_2006_02
□ ✎ ✗	Murray, Dan	Fontax	1A8	Mitsou 2007	3	4
□ ✎ ✗	Murray, Dan	Fontax	2X12	Wanderer 2006	7	0
□ ✎ ✗	Smith, Peter	Licorne	LKC	Gazelle 2007	1	6
□ ✎ ✗	Smith, Peter	Fontax	1A8	Mitsou 2007	1	0

However this structure has many maintenance problems. For instance, where do we store the figures for March 2006? To discover some of the other problems, let's examine sample SQL statements we could use on this table to query about specific questions, followed by the results of those statements:

```
/* displays the maximum number of cars of a single model sold by each
vendor in January 2006 */
SELECT salesperson, max(qty_2006_01)
FROM sales
GROUP BY salesperson
```

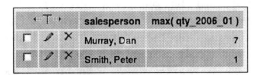

←T→	salesperson	max(qty_2006_01)
□ ✎ ✗	Murray, Dan	7
□ ✎ ✗	Smith, Peter	1

```
/* finds the average number of cars sold by our sales force taken as a
whole, in February 2006 */
SELECT avg(qty_2006_02)
FROM sales
WHERE qty_2006_02 > 0
```

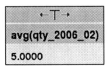

←T→
avg(qty_2006_02)
5.0000

```
/* finds for which model more than three cars were sold in January */
SELECT model_name_year, SUM(qty_2006_01)
FROM sales
GROUP BY model_name_year
HAVING SUM(qty_2006_01) > 3
```

model_name_year	SUM(qty_2006_01)
Mitsou 2007	4
Wanderer 2006	7

We notice that, although we got the answers we were looking for, with the above SQL queries, we would have to modify column names in the queries to obtain results for other months. Also, it becomes tricky if we want to know the month for which the sales have surpassed the yearly average, because we have to potentially deal with twelve column names. Another problem would arise when attempting to report for different years, or to compare a year with another one.

Moreover, a situation that could demonstrate the poor state of this structure is the need for a new report. A structure that is based too closely on a single report instead of being based on the intrinsic relations between data elements does not scale well and fails to accommodate future needs.

Chapter 4 will unfold those problems.

Summary

We saw that MySQL's popularity has put a powerful tool on the desktop of many users; some of them are not on par about design techniques. Data is an important resource and we have to think about the organization's data as a whole. The powerful relational model can help us for structuring activities. This book avoids specialized, academic vocabulary about the relational model, focusing instead on the important principles and the minimum tasks needed to produce a good structure. We then saw our main case study, and we noticed how it's unfortunately easy to build wide, inefficient tables.

2
Data Collecting

In order to structure data, one must first gather data elements and establish the domain to which this data applies. This chapter deals with raw data information that comes from the users or other sources, and the techniques that can help us to build a comprehensive data collection. This collection will become our input for all further activities like data naming and grouping.

To be able to build a data collection, we will first identify the limits of the system. This will be followed by gathering documents in order to find significant data elements. The next step will be to conduct interviews with key users in order to refine the list of data elements. All these steps are described in this chapter.

System Boundaries Identification

Let's establish the scenario. We have been called by a local car dealer to submit a proposal about a new information system. The stated goal is to produce reports about car sales and to help track the car inventory. Reports are, of course, an output of the future system. The idea hidden behind reports could be to improve sales, to understand delivery delays, or to find out why some cars disappear. The data structure itself is probably not really important in the users' opinion, but we know that this structure matters to the developers who produce the required output.

It's important to first look at the project scope, before starting to work on the details of the system. Does the project cover:

- The complete enterprise
- Just one administrative area
- Multiple administrative areas
- One function of the enterprise

An organization always has a main purpose; it can be selling cars, teaching, or providing web solutions. In addition to this, every organization has sub-activities like human resource management, payroll, and marketing. The approach to data collecting will vary, depending upon the exact area we are dealing with. Let's say we learn that our car dealer also operates a repair shop, which has its own inventory, along with a car rental service. Do we include these inventories in our analyzing tasks? We have to correctly understand the place of this new information system in its context.

When preparing a data model, the biggest challenge is probably to draw a line, to clearly state where to stop. This is challenging for various reasons:

- Our user might have only a vague idea of what they want, of the benefits they expect from the new system
- Conflicting interests might exist between our future users; some of them might want to prioritize issues in a different way from others, maybe because they are involved with the tedious tasks that the new system promises to eliminate
- We might be tempted to improve enterprise-wide information flow beyond the scope of this particular project

It's not an easy task to balance user-perceived goals with the needs of the organization as a whole.

Modular Development

It is generally admitted that breaking a problem or task into smaller parts helps us to focus on more manageable units and, in the long run, permits us to achieve a better solution, and a complete solution. Having smaller segments means that defining each part's purpose is simpler and that the testing process is easier – as a smaller segment contains less details. This is why, when establishing the system boundaries, we should think in terms of developing by modules. In our case study, a simple way of dividing into modules would be the following:

- Module 1: car sales
- Module 2: car inventory

Delivering an information system in incremental steps can help reassure the customer about the final product. Defining the modules and a schedule about them can motivate users and also the developers. With a publicized schedule, everyone knows what to expect.

With the idea of modules comes the idea of budget and the notion of priorities for development. Do we have to deliver the car sales module before or after the inventory module? Can those modules be done separately? Are there some constraints that must be addressed, like a new report about the car sales that the Chief Executive Officer (CEO) needs by June 20? Another point to take into account is how the modules are related. Chances are good that some data will be shared between modules, so the data model prepared for module 1 will probably be reused and refined during module 2 developments.

Model Flexibility

Another point not directly related to our user but to us as developers is: can the data model be built to be flexible and more general? This way, it could be applied to other car dealers, always keeping in mind contract issues between the developer and the user. (Who will own the work?) Should the data structure be developed with other sales domains in mind? For instance, this could lead to a table named goods instead of cars. Maybe this kind of generalization can help, maybe not, because data elements description must always remain clear.

Document Gathering

This step can be done before the interviews. The goal is to gather documents about this organization and start designing our questions for the interviews. Of course, a data model for car sales has some things in common with other sales systems, but there is a special culture about cars. Another set of documents will be collected during the interviews while we learn about the forms used by the interviewees.

General Reading

Here are some reading suggestions:

- Enterprise annual report
- Corporate goals statement
- President's speech
- Publicity material
- Bulletin board

I once learned a lot about information flow from a grocery store's bulletin board for the employees. There were small notes from management to employees explaining how to handle clients who pay by cheque (which personal information must be obtained from the client before the store can accept their cheque), and detailing the schedule for sick employees' replacement. Also explained on the board, was the procedure to use on the cash register to give reward points to clients who pay with the store's credit card. This information is sometimes more useful than an annual report because we are seeking details from the persons who are involved with the daily tasks.

Forms

The forms, which represent paperwork between the enterprise and external partners, or between internal departments, should be scrutinized. They can reveal a massive amount of data, even if further analysis shows unused, imprecise, or redundant data. Many organizations suffer from the *form disease* – a tendency to use too many paper or screen forms and to produce too complex forms. Nonetheless, if we are able to look at the forms currently used to convey information about the car inventory or car sales, for example, a purchase order from the car dealer to the manufacturer, we might find on these forms essential data about the purchase that will be useful to complete our data collection.

Existing Computerized Systems

The car dealer has already started sales operations a number of years ago. To support these sales, they were probably using some kind of computerized system, even if this could have been only a spreadsheet. This pre-existing system surely contains interesting data elements. We should try to have a look at this existing information system, if one exists, and if we are allowed to. Regarding the data structuring process itself, we can learn about some data elements that are not seen on the paper forms. Also, this can help when the time comes to implement a new system by easing transition and training.

Interviews

The goal for conducting interviews is to learn about the vocabulary pertaining to the studied system. This book is about data structures, but the information gathered during the interviews can surely help in subsequent activities of the system's development like coding, testing, and refinements.

Interviews are a critical part of the whole process. In our example, a customer asked for a system about car sales and inventory tracking. At this point, many users cannot explain further what they want. The problem is exactly this: how can I, as a developer, find out what they want? After the interview phase, things become clearer since we will have gathered data elements. Moreover, often the customer who ordered a new system does not grasp the data flow's full picture; it might also happen that this customer won't be the one who will work with all aspects of the system, those which are more targeted towards clerical persons.

Finding the Right Users

The suggested approach would be to contact the best person for the questions about the new system. Sometimes, the person in charge insists that *he/she* is the best person, it might be true, or not. This can become delicate, especially if we finally meet someone who knows better, even if this is during an informal meeting.

Thinking about the following issues can help to find the best candidates:

- Who wants this system built?
- Who will profit from it?
- Which users would be most cooperative?

Evidently, this can lead to meeting with several people to explore the various sub-domains. Some of these domains might intersect, with a potential negative impact – diverging opinions, or with a potential positive impact – validating facts with more than one interviewee.

Perceptions

During the interviews, we will meet different kinds of users. Some of these will be very knowledgeable about the processes involved with the car dealer's activities, for example, meeting with a potential customer, inviting them for a test drive, and ordering a car. Some other users will only know a part of the whole process, their knowledge scope is limited. Due to the varying scope, we will hear different perceptions about the same subject.

For example, talking about how to identify a car, we will hear diverging opinions. Some will want to identify a car with its serial number; others will want to use their own in-house car number. They all refer to the same car with a different angle. These various opinions will have to be reconciled later when proceeding with the data naming phase.

Asking the Right Questions

There are various ways to consider which questions are relevant and which will enable us to gather significant data elements.

Existing Information Systems

Is there an existing information system: manual or computerized? What will happen with this existing system? Either we export relevant data from this existing system to feed the new one, to completely do away with the old system, or we keep the existing system – temporarily or permanently.

If we must keep the existing system, we'll probably build a bridge between the two systems for exchanging data. In this case, do we need a one-way bridge or a two-way bridge?

Chronological Events

Who orders a car for the show room and why; how is the order made – phone, fax, email, website; can a car in the showroom be sold to a customer?

Sources and Destinations

Here we question about information, money, bills, goods, and services. For example, what is the source of a car? What's its destination? Is the buyer of a car always an individual, or can it be another company?

Urgency

Thinking about the current way in which you deal with information, which problems do you consider the most urgent to solve?

Avoid Focusing on Reports and Screens

An approach too centered on the (perceived) needs of the users may lead to gaps in the data structure, because each user does not necessarily have an accurate vision of all their needs or all the needs of other users. It's quite rare in an enterprise to find someone who grasps the whole data picture, with the complex inter-departmental interactions that frequently occur.

This bias will show up during the interviews. Users are usually more familiar with items they can see or visualize and less familiar with concepts. However, there are distinctions between the user interface (UI) and the underlying data. UI design considers ergonomic and aesthetic issues, whereas data structuring has to follow different, non-visual rules to be effective.

Data Collected for our Case Study

Here is a list, jotted down during the interviews, of potential data elements and details which seem important to the current information flow. It's very important during this collection to note, not only the data elements' names – shall we say "provisional names" at this point – but also sample values. The benefit of this will become apparent in Chapter 3. In the following data collection, we include sample values in brackets where appropriate.

From the General Manager

Our friend the General Manager keeps surveys filled by buyers about their buying experience as a whole. Those surveys contain remarks about the salesperson behavior. Evidently, this information is confidential, as only the General Manager and the office clerk have access to it. Survey information includes:

- Date: (2006-01-02)
- Salesperson's name: (Harper, Paul)
- Buyer's name: (Smith, Joe)
- The points to evaluate: courtesy, quality of information given, etc
- For each point, the mark given by the buyer from one to ten.

From the Salesperson

The main form prepared by a salesperson is the Sales Contract, and this person surely hopes to prepare plenty of these! Here are the elements present on the Sales Contract:

- Buyer's information: name, address, postal code, phone number
- Dealer's information: name, address, postal code, phone number
- Salesperson information: name, address, postal code, phone number
- Quantity of vehicles for this sale (usually 1)
- Car description: brand, model, year (Fontax Mitsou 2007)
- Car condition: new/used
- Car serial number: (D34HTT987)
- Car color: (aquamarine)
- Selling price: (32,500)
- Insurance company name: (MicMac Car Insurance Inc.)
- Insurance policy number: (J44-5764, but each company has its own code system for this)
- Preparation cost: (800)
- Tax amount: (2,400)
- Total price: (35,700)
- Vehicle giving in exchange:
    - brand: (Licorne)
    - model: (Wanderer)

- ° year: (2006)
- ° serial number: (D45TGH45738)
- ° price of the exchange: (12,000)

- Down payment: (4,000)
- Interest rate: (9%)
- Interest amount: (6345)
- Type of credit rate: fixed/variable
- Dates of first and last payments: (2007-07-01, 2011-06-01)
- Number of payments: (48)
- Financial institution's information: name, address, postal code, phone number

From the Store Assistant

A store assistant assigns a car number to each vehicle that enters the floor. This helps to manage which set of keys belongs to which car, we refer to physical keys here – the keys needed to unlock and start the car, not the database keys. The car number does not refer to the car's serial number; it's assigned sequentially and used internally only.

Store assistants also prepare a delivery certificate which contains the following information:

- Buyer's name: (Joe Smith)
- Dealer's number: (53119)
- Vehicle id number: (1400)
- Key number: (81947)
- Four signatures and dates, from the buyer, general manager, salesperson, and the store assistant

Finally, the store assistants keep a register about all car movements. For each car, a card-index contains:

- Id number of the car: (432)
- Car ordered: date (2007-02-03)
- Car arrived: date (2007-02-17)
- Car placed in the show room: date (2007-02-19)
- Car washed: date (2007-05-30)

- Car gas tank filled-up: date (2007-05-30)
- Car delivered to buyer: date (2007-06-01)

Other Notes

- Do we include in the model some information about the old car that the customer exchanges for their new car?
- Boundary: during the interviews it was decided that, for now, the model will not include the dealer's car rental activities, nor their repair service, although much of the information about cars could be applied to those activities.

The subsequent chapters will put order in the naming aspects of this data and will explain grouping techniques.

Summary

Building a comprehensive collection of data elements is essential to the success of a data structuring activity. However, we need to know the exact limits of the analyzed system. Then, by gathering documents and proceeding with interview activities, we can record a list of potential data elements – our future column names.

3
Data Naming

In this chapter, we focus on transforming the data elements gathered in the collection process into a cohesive set of column names. Although this chapter has sections for the various steps we should accomplish for efficient data naming, there is no specific order in which to apply those steps. In fact, the whole process is broken down into steps to shed some light on each one in turn, but the actual naming process applies all those steps at the same time. Moreover, the division between the naming and grouping processes is somewhat artificial – you'll see that some decisions about naming influence the grouping phase, which is the subject of the next chapter.

Data Cleaning

Having gathered information elements from various sources, some cleaning work is appropriate to improve the significance of these elements. The way each interviewee named elements might be inconsistent; moreover, the significance of a term can vary from person to person. Thus, a synonym detection process is in order.

Since we took note of sample values, now it is time to cross-reference our list of elements with those sample values. Here is a practical example, using the car's id number.

When the decision is made to order a car – a Mitsou 2007 – the office clerk opens a new file and assigns a sequential number dubbed `car_id` number to the file, for instance, 725. At this point, no confirmation has been received from any car supplier, so the clerk does not know the future car's serial number – a unique number stamped on the engine and other critical parts of the vehicle.

This car's id number is referred to as the `car_number` by the office clerk. The store assistants who register car movements use the name `stock_number`. But using this car number or the stock number is not meaningful for financing and insurance purposes; the car's serial number is used instead for that purpose.

At this point, a consensus must be reached by convincing users about the importance of standard terms. It must become clear to everyone that the term `car_number` is not precise enough to be used, so it will be replaced by `car_internal_number` in the data elements list, probably also in any user interface (UI) or report.

It can be argued that `car_internal_number` should be replaced by something more appropriate; the important point here is we merged two synonyms: `car_number` and `stock_number`, and established the difference between two elements that looked similar but were not, eliminating a source of confusion.

Therefore we end up with the following elements:

- `Car_serial_number`
- `Car_internal_number` (former car id number and stock number)

Eventually, when dealing with data grouping, another decision will have to be taken: to which number, serial or internal, do we associate the car's physical key number.

Subdividing Data Elements

In this section, we try to find out if some elements should be broken into more simple ones. The reason for doing so is that, if an element is composed of many parts, applications will have to break it for sorting and selection purposes. Thus it's better to break the elements right now at the source. Recomposing it will be easier at the application level.

Breaking the elements provides more clarity at the UI level. Therefore, at this level we will avoid (as much as possible) the well-known last-name/first-name inversion problem.

As an example for this problem, let's take the buyer's name. During the interview, we noticed that the name is expressed in various ways on the forms:

Form	How the name is expressed
Delivery certificate	Mr Joe Smith
Sales contract	Smith, Joe

We notice that

- There is a salutation element, Mr
- The element name is too imprecise; we really have a first name and a last name
- On the sales contract, the comma after our last name should really be excluded from the element, as it's only a formatting character

As a result, we determine that we should sub-divide the name into the following elements:

- Salutation
- First name
- Last name

Sometimes it's useful to sub-divide an element, sometimes it's not. Let's consider the date elements. We could sub-divide each one into year, month, and day (three integers) but by doing so, we would lose the date calculation possibilities that MySQL offers. Among those are, finding the week day from a date, or determining the date that falls thirty days after a certain date. So for the date (and time), a single column can handle it all, although at the UI level, separate entry fields should be displayed for year, month, and day. This is to avoid any possibility of mix-up and also because we cannot expect users to know about what MySQL accepts as a valid date. There is a certain latitude in the range of valid values but we can take it for granted that users have unlimited creativity, regarding how to enter invalid values. If a single field is present on the UI, clear directions should be provided to help with filling this field correctly.

Data Elements Containing Formatting Characters

The last case we'll examine is the phone number. In many parts of the world, the phone number follows a specific pattern and also uses formatting characters for legibility. In North America, we have a regional code, an exchange number, and phone number, for example, 418-111-2222; an extension could possibly be appended to the phone number. However, in practice only the regional code and extension are separated from the rest into data elements of their own. Moreover, people often enter formatting characters like (418) 111-2222 and expect those to be output back. So, a standard output format must be chosen, and then the correct number of sub-elements will have to be set into the model to be able to recreate the expected output.

Data that are Results

Even though it might seem natural to have a distinct element for the `total_price` of the car, in practice this is not justified. The reason is that the total price is a computed result. Having the total price printed on a sales contract constitutes an output. Thus, we eliminate this information in the list of column names. For the same reason, we could omit the `tax` column because it can be computed.

By removing the total price column, we could encounter a pitfall. We have to be sure that we can reconstruct this total price from other sub-total elements, now and in the future. This might not be possible for a number of reasons:

- The total price includes an amount located in another table, and this table will change over time (for example, the tax rate). To avoid this problem, see the recommendations in the *Scalability over Time* section in Chapter 4.

- This total price contains an arbitrary value, due to some exceptional cases, for example, where there is a special sale, and the rebate was not planned in the system, or when the lucky buyer is the brother-in-law of the general manager! In this case, a decision can be made: adding a new column `other_rebate`.

Data as a Column's or Table's Name

Now is the time to uncover what is perhaps the least known of the data naming problems: data hidden in a column's or even a table's name.

We had one example of this in Chapter 1. Remember the `qty_2006_1` column name. Although this is a commonly seen mistake, it's a mistake nonetheless. We clearly have two ideas here, the quantity and the date. Of course, to be able to use just two columns, some work will have to be done regarding the keys – this is covered in Chapter 4. For now, we should just use elements like `quantity` and `date` in our elements list, avoiding representing data in a column's name.

To find those problematic cases in our model, a possible method is to look for numbers. Column names like `address1`, `address2` or `phone1`, `phone2` should look suspicious.

Now, have a look in Chapter 2 at the data elements we got from our store assistant. Can you find a case of data being hidden in a column name?

If you have done this exercise, you might have found many past participles hidden into the column names, like *ordered*, *arrived*, and *washed*. These describe the events that happen to a car. We could try to anticipate all possible events but it might prove impossible. Who knows when a new column `car_provided_with_big_ribbon` will be needed? Such events, if treated as distinct column names, must be addressed by

- A change in the data structure
- A change in the code (UI and reports)

To stay flexible and avoid the wide-table syndrome, we need two tables: `car_event` and `event`.

Here are the structure and sample values for those tables:

```
CREATE TABLE `event` (
  `code` int(11) NOT NULL,
  `description` char(40) NOT NULL,
  PRIMARY KEY  ('code')
) ENGINE=MyISAM DEFAULT CHARSET=latin1;

INSERT INTO `event` VALUES (1, 'washed');
```

 The usage of backticks here ('event'), although not standard SQL, is a MySQL extension used to enclose and protect identifiers. In this specific case, it could help us with MySQL 5.1 in which the event keyword is scheduled to become part of the language for some another purpose (CREATE EVENT). At the time of writing, beta version MySQL 5.1.11 accepts CREATE TABLE event, but it might not always be true.

The following image shows sample values entered into the event table from within the **Insert** sub-page of phpMyAdmin:

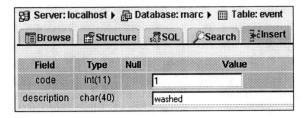

```
CREATE TABLE `car_event` (
  `internal_number` int(11) NOT NULL,
  `moment` datetime NOT NULL,
  `event_code` int(11) NOT NULL,
  PRIMARY KEY  ('internal_number')
) ENGINE=MyISAM DEFAULT CHARSET=latin1;

INSERT INTO `car_event` VALUES (412, '2006-05-20 09:58:38', 1);
```

Again, sample values are entered via phpMyAdmin:

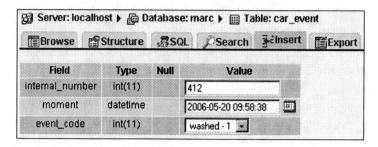

Data can also hide in a table name. Let's consider the `car` and `truck` tables. They should probably be merged into a `vehicle` table, since the vehicle's category – truck, car, and other values like minivan is really an attribute of a particular vehicle. We could also find another case for this table name problem: a table named `vehicle_1996`.

Planning for Changes

When designing a data structure, we have to think about how to manage its growth and the possible implications of the chosen technique.

Let's say an unplanned car characteristic – the weight – has to be supported. The normal way of solving this is to find the proper table and add a column. Indeed, this is the best solution; however, someone has to alter the table's structure, and probably the UI too.

The **free fields technique**, also called second-level data or **EAV** (Entity-Attribute-Value) technique is sometimes used in this case. To summarize this technique, we use a column whose value is a column name by itself.

 Even if this technique is shown here, I do not recommend using it, for the reasons explained in the *Pitfalls of the Free Fields Technique* section below.

The difference between this technique and our `car_event` table is that, for `car_event`, the various attributes can all be related to a common subject, which is the event. On the contrary, free fields can store any kind of dissimilar data. This might also be a way to store data specific to a single instance or row of a table.

In the following example, we use the `car_free_field` table to store unplanned information about the car whose `internal_number` is 412. The weight and special paint had not been planned, so the UI gave the user the chance to specify which information they want to keep, and the corresponding value. We see here a screenshot from phpMyAdmin but most probably, another UI would be presented to the user – for example the salesperson who might not be trained to play at the database level.

```
CREATE TABLE `car_free_field` (
  `internal_number` int(11) NOT NULL,
  `free_name` varchar(30) NOT NULL,
  `free_value` varchar(30) NOT NULL,
  PRIMARY KEY  ('internal_number','free_name')
) ENGINE=MyISAM DEFAULT CHARSET=latin1;

INSERT INTO `car_free_field` VALUES (412, 'weight', '2000');
INSERT INTO `car_free_field` VALUES (412, 'special paint needed',
'gold');
```

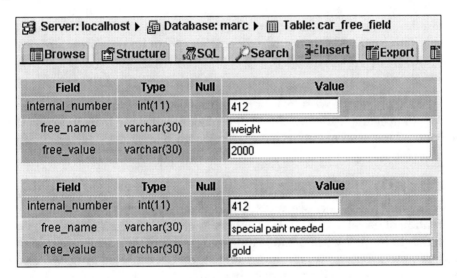

Pitfalls of the Free Fields Technique

Even if it's tempting to use this kind of table for added flexibility and to avoid user interface maintenance, there are a number of reasons why we should avoid using it.

- It becomes impossible to link this "column" (for example the **special paint needed**) to a lookup table containing the possible colors, with a foreign key constraint.

- The `free_value` field itself must be defined with a generic field type like `VARCHAR` whose size must be wide enough to accommodate all values for all possible corresponding `free_name` values.

- It prevents easy validation (for a weight, we need a numeric value).

- Coding the SQL queries on these free fields becomes more complex – i.e. `SELECT internal_number from car_free_field where free_name = 'weight' and free_value > 2000`.

Naming Recommendations

Here we touch a subject that can become sensitive. Establishing a naming convention is not easily done, because it can interfere with the psychology of the designers.

Designer's Creativity

Programmers and designers usually think of themselves as imaginative, creative people; UI design and data model are the areas in which they want to express those qualities. Since naming is writing, they want to put a personal stamp to the column and table names. This is why working as a team for data structure design necessitates a good dose of humility and achieves good results only if everyone is a good team player.

Also, when looking at the work of others in this area, there is a great temptation to *improve* the data elements names. Some discipline in the standardization has to be applied and all the team members have to collaborate.

Abbreviations

Probably because older database systems had severe restrictions about the representation of variables and data elements in general, the practice of abbreviating has been taught for many years and is followed by many data structure designers and programmers. I used programming languages that accepted only two characters for variable names – we had to extensively comment the correspondence between those cropped variables and their meaning.

Nowadays, I see no valid reasons for systematically abbreviating all column and table names; after all, who will understand the meaning of your `T1` table or your `B7` field?

Clarity versus Length: an Art

A consistent style of abbreviations should be used. In general, only the most meaningful words of a sentence should be put into a name, dropping prepositions, and other small words. As an example, let's take the postal code. We could express this element with different column names:

- the_postal_code
- pstl_code
- pstlcd
- postal_code

I recommend the last one for its simplicity.

Suffixing

Carefully chosen suffixes can add clarity to column names. As an example, for the *date of first payment* element, I would suggest `first_payment_date`. In fact, the last word of a column name is often used to describe the type of content – like `customer_no`, `color_code`, `interest_amount`.

The Plural Form

Another point of controversy for table names: should we use the plural form `cars` table? It can be argued that the answer is yes because this table contains many cars – in other words, it is a set. Nonetheless, I tend not to use the plural form for the simple reason that it adds nothing in terms of information. I know that a table is a set, so using the plural form would be redundant. It can be said also that each row describes one car.

If we consider the subject on the angle of queries, we can draw different conclusions depending on the query. A query referring to the car table – `select car.color_code from car where car.id = 34` is more elegant if the plural form is not used, because the main idea here is that we retrieve one car whose id equals 34. Some other queries might make more sense with a plural, like `select count(*) from cars`.

As a conclusion for this section, the debate is not over, but the most important point is to choose a form and be consistent throughout the whole system.

Naming Consistency

We should ensure that a data element that is present in more than one table is represented everywhere by the same column name. In MySQL, a column name does not exist by itself; it is always inside a table. This is why, unfortunately, we cannot pick up consistent column names from, say, a pool of standardized column names and associate it with the tables. Instead, during each table's creation we indicate the exact column names we want and their attributes. So, let's avoid using different names – `internal_number` and `internal_num` when they refer to the same reality.

An exception for this: if the column's name refers to a key in another table – the `state` column – and we have more than one column referring to it like `state_of_birth, `state_of_residence``.

MySQL's Possibilities versus Portability

MySQL permits the use of many more characters for identifiers – database, table, and column names than its competitors. The blank space is accepted as are accented characters. The simple trade-off is that we need to enclose such special names with back quotes like `'state of residence'`. This procures a great liberty in the expression of data elements, especially for non-English designers, but introduces a state of non-portability because those identifiers are not accepted in standard SQL. Even some SQL implementations only accept uppercase characters for identifiers.

I recommend being very prudent before deciding to include such characters. Even when staying faithful to MySQL, there has been a portability issue between versions earlier than 4.1 when upgrading to 4.1. In 4.1.x, MySQL started to represent identifiers internally in UTF-8 code, so a renaming operation had to be done to ensure that no accented characters in the database, table, column and constraint names were present before the upgrade. This tedious operation is not very practical in a 24/7 system availability context.

Table Name into a Column Name

Another style I often see: one would systematically add the table name as a prefix to every column name. Thus the `car` table would be comprised of the columns: `car_id_number, car_serial_number`. I think this is redundant and it shows its inelegance when examining the queries we build:

```
select car_id_number from car
```

is not too bad, but when joining tables we get a query such as

```
select car.car_id_number,
buyer.buyer_name
from car, buyer
```

Since at the application level, the majority of queries we code are multi-tables like the one used above, the clumsiness of using a table name even abbreviated as part of column names becomes readily apparent. Of course, the same exception we saw in the *Naming Consistency* section applies: a column – foreign key – referring to a lookup table normally includes this table's name as part of the column's name. For example, in the `car_event` table, we have `event_code` which refers to the `code` column in table `event`.

Summary

To get a clear and understandable data structure, proper data elements naming is important. We examined many techniques to apply in order to build consistent table and column names.

4

Data Grouping

In the previous chapters, we built a data collection, and started to clean it by proper naming. We had already introduced, in Chapter 1, the notion of a table, which logically regroups information about a certain subject. Some of the columns we gathered were grouped into tables during the naming process. While doing so, we noticed that the process of name checking was sometimes leading us to decompose data into more tables, like we did for the `car_event` and `event` tables. The goal of the present chapter is to provide finishing touches to our structure, by examining the technique of grouping column names into tables. Our data elements won't be living "in the air"; they will have to be organized into tables. Exactly which columns must be placed into which table will be considered here.

Initial List of Tables

When building the structure, we can start by finding general, natural subjects which look promising for grouping data. These subjects will provide our initial list of tables – here is an abridged example of what this list might look like:

- vehicle
- customer
- event
- vehicle sale
- customer satisfaction survey

We'll begin our columns grouping work by considering the `vehicle` table.

Rules for Table Layout

There can be more than one correct solution, but any correct solution will tend to respect the following principles:

- each table has a primary key
- no redundant data is present when considering all tables as a whole
- all columns in a table depend directly upon all segments of the primary key

These principles will be studied in details in the following sections.

Primary Keys and Table Names

Let's start by defining the concept of a **unique key**. A column on which a unique key is defined cannot hold the same value more than once for this table. The **primary key** is composed of one or more columns, it is a value that can be used to identify a unique row in a table. Why do we need a primary key? MySQL itself does not force us to have a primary key, neither a unique key nor any other kind of key, for a specific table. Thus MySQL puts us under no obligation to follow Codd's rules. However, in practice it's important to have a primary key; experience acquired while building web interfaces and other applications shows that it's very useful to be able to refer to a key identifying a row in a unique way. In MySQL, a primary key is a unique key where all columns have to be defined as NOT NULL; the name of this key is PRIMARY. Choosing the primary key is done almost at the same time as choosing the table's name.

Selecting the name of our tables is a delicate process. We have to be general enough to provide for future expansion – like the vehicle table instead of car and truck. At the same time, we try to avoid having holes – empty columns in our tables.

To decide if we should have a vehicle table or two separate tables, we look at the possible attributes for each kind of vehicle. Are they common enough? Both vehicle types have a color, a model, a year, a serial number, and an internal id number. Theoretically, the list of columns must be identical for us to decide that a group of columns will belong to a single table; but we can cheat a bit, if there are only a few attributes that are different.

Let's say we decide to have a vehicle table. For reasons explained earlier, we want to track a vehicle since the moment we order it – we'll use its internal id number as the primary key. When designing this table, we ask ourselves whether this table can be used to store information about the vehicles we receive in exchange from the customer. The answer is *yes*, since describing a vehicle has nothing to do with the transactions that happen to it (new vehicle sold, used vehicle bought from the customer). The section *Validating the Structure* gives further examples that can help catching problems in the structure. Here is version 1 of the vehicle table, with column names and sample values – we mark the columns comprising the primary key with an asterisk:

table: vehicle	column name	sample value
	*internal_id	123
	serial_number	D8894JF
	brand	Licorne
	model	Gazelle
	year	2007
	color	ocean blue
	condition	new

Should we include the sales info, for example, pricing and date of sale, in this table? We determine that the answer is *no* since a number of things can happen:

- the vehicle can be resold
- the table might be used to hold information about a vehicle received in exchange

We now have to examine our work and verify that we have respected the principles. We have a primary key, but what about redundancy and dependency?

Data Redundancy and Dependency

Whenever possible, we should evacuate redundant data into lookup tables – also called reference tables and store only the value of the codes into our main tables. We don't want to repeat "Licorne" into our vehicle table for each Licorne sold. Redundant data wastes disk space and increases processing time when doing database maintenance: if a modification need arises, all instances of the same data must be updated. Regarding the `vehicle` table, it would be redundant to store a full descriptive value in the `brand`, `model` and `color` columns – storing three codes will suffice.

We have to be careful about evacuating redundant data. For example, we won't be coding the year; this would be too much coding for no saving – using A for 2006, B for 2007 makes no practical saving of space after a few thousand years! Even for a small number of years, the space saving would not be significant; beside, we would lose the ability to do computations on the year.

Next, we verify dependency. Each column must be dependent on the primary key. Is the condition new/used directly dependent on the vehicle? No, if we consider it over the time dimension. In theory, the dealer can sell a car, and then accept it later in exchange. The condition is related more to the transaction itself, for a specific date, so it really belongs to the sale table – shown here in a non-final state. We now have version 2:

table: vehicle	column name	sample value
	*internal_id	123
	serial_number	D8894JF
	brand_code	L
	model_code	G
	year	2007
	color_code	1A6

table: brand	column name	sample value
	*code	L
	description	Licorne

table: model	column name	sample value
	*code	G
	description	Gazelle

table: color	column name	sample value
	*code	1A6
	description	ocean blue

table: sale	column name	sample value
	*date	2006-03-17
	*internal_id	123
	condition_code	N

Composite Keys

A **composite key**, also called as compound key, is a key that consists of more than one column.

When laying out our code tables, we must verify that the data grouping principles are also respected on those tables. Using sample data, and also our imagination to supplement incomplete sample data, can help to uncover problems in this area. In our version 2, we overlooked one possibility. What if the companies marketing two different brands chose an identical color code 1A6 to represent different colors? The same could happen for model codes so we should refine the structure to include the brand code – which represents Fontax, Licorne or a future brand name – into the `model` and `color` tables. Thus version 3 displays the two tables that have changed from version 2:

table: model	column name	sample value
	*brand_code	L
	*code	G
	description	Gazelle

table: color	column name	sample value
	*brand_code	L
	*code	1A6
	description	ocean blue

Both the `model` and `color` tables result in having a composite key. Another example of a composite key was seen in Chapter 3: the `car_event` table – see the *Data as a Column's or Table's name* section. In these kinds of tables, the primary key is composed of more than one element. This happens when we have to describe data that relates to more than one table. Usually, the newly formed table for `car_event` containing the car internal number and the event code has further attributes like the date when a specific event occurs for a specific car.

Another possibility for a composite key arises when we encounter subsets like a department of a company. Associating an employee id to just the company code or just the department code would not describe the situation correctly. An employee id is unique only when considering both the department and the company.

We have to verify that all the non-key data elements of this table depend directly upon the key taken in its entirety. Here is a problematic case where the `company_name` column is misplaced because it's not related to `dept_code`:

table: company_dept	column name	sample value
	*company_code	1
	*dept_code	16
	dept_name	Marketing
	company_name	Fontax

The previous example is non-optimal because the company name would be present in every row of a table intended to describe each department. The correct structure for the previous example implies the use of two tables:

table: dept	column name	sample value
	*company_code	1
	*code	16
	name	Marketing

table: company	column name	sample value
	*code	1
	name	Fontax

Improving the Structure

Even when our table layout respects the rules, we can still refine it by looking at the following additional issues.

Scalability over Time

In Chapter 3 (section *Data that are Results*), we saw that we could avoid reserving a column for the tax amount, provided we have the exact tax rate in a reference table. However this rate could change so we need a more complete table that contains date ranges and the corresponding rate. This way, projecting the system over the time dimension, we can ensure that it will accommodate rate fluctuations. Note that the following sale table is not complete:

table: sale	column name	sample value
	*date	2006-03-17
	*internal_id	123
	condition_code	N

table: condition	column name	sample value
	*code	N
	description	New

Comparing the `date` column from the `sale` table with the `start_date` and `end_date` from the following `tax_rate` table, we can find the exact tax rate for the date of sale:

table: tax_rate	column name	sample value
	*start_date	2006-01-01
	*end_date	2006-04-01
	rate	.075

In fact, all tables should be analysed to find whether the time factor has been considered. Another example would be the `color` table. Assuming we are using the color codes designed by each car manufacturer, does a manufacturer reuse color codes in a subsequent year for a different color? If this is the case, we would add a `year` column to the `color` table.

Empty Columns

Although empty columns are not necessarily problematic, having some rows where one or many columns are empty can reveal a structural problem: two tables folded into one. Let's consider the car movements. We built a structure having a car's internal number, the code of the event, and the moment. But what if some events need more data to be described?

In the paper forms, we discover that when a car is washed, the initials of the store assistant who did the washing appear on the form, and during the interviews, we learned that these initials are an important data element.

In this case, we can add employee information, the employee code, to the `car_event` table. This would have the benefit of enabling the system to identify which store assistant participated to any event occurring to a car, leading to better quality control.

Another issue that might arise is that for a specific event (say washing) we require more data more data like the quantity of cleaning product, and the amount of time used to wash. Of those two elements, one can be beneficial to improve our structure: storing the start and end time of the event. But adding a column like **quantity_cleaning_product** to the `car_event` table has to be analyzed carefully. For all events except washing, this column would remain empty, leading to exception treatment in the applications. The structure would only worsen if we added another column related to another special event.

←T→	internal_number	moment	event_code	quantity_cleaning_product
□ ✎ ✗	412	2006-05-20 09:58:38	2	0
□ ✎ ✗	500	2006-05-29 16:37:46	1	12
□ ✎ ✗	600	2006-05-30 16:38:51	washed	0
□ ✎ ✗	700	2006-05-31 16:39:21	2	0

In this case, it's better to create another table with the same keys and the additional columns. We cannot avoid having some data elements in this new table name: car_washing_event.

table: car_washing_event	column name	sample value
	*internal_number	412
	quantity_cleaning_product	12

Avoiding ENUM and SET

MySQL and SQL in general offer what looks like convenient data types: ENUM and SET types. Both types permit us to specify a list of possible values for a column, along with a default value; the difference being that a SET column can hold multiple values, whereas an ENUM can contain only one of the potential values.

We see here a very small sale table with the credit_rate column being an ENUM:

```
CREATE TABLE `sale` (
  `internal_number` int(11) NOT NULL,
  `date` date NOT NULL,
  `credit_rate` ENUM('fixed','variable') NOT NULL,
  PRIMARY KEY  (`internal_number`)
) ENGINE=MyISAM DEFAULT CHARSET=latin1;
```

When a field is defined as ENUM or SET and we are using phpMyAdmin's insertion or data edit panels, a dropdown list of the values is displayed so it might be tempting to use those data types.

Server: localhost ▸	Database: marc ▸	Table: sale				

Browse	Structure	SQL	Search	Insert	Export	Import

Field	Type	Function	Null	Value
internal_number	int(11)			
sale_date	date			
credit_rate	enum	--		

fixed
variable

Let's examine the benefits of such types:

- Instead of storing the complete value, MySQL stores only an integer index, which uses one or two bytes, depending on the number of values in the list
- MySQL itself refuses any value that is not comprised in the list

Even after considering these benefits, it is recommended not to use ENUM and SET types for the following reasons:

- Changing the list of possible values needs a developer action, such as a structure modification intervention
- There are limits for those types: 65535 possible values in the list; also a SET can have 64 active members, which are the chosen values in the set
- It's better to keep the system more simple, because if in some cases we use lookup tables and in other cases ENUM or SET types, the program code is more complex to build and maintain

It could be argued that problem number one can be solved by including in the application some ALTER TABLE statements to change the list of values, but this does not seem the normal way to deal with this matter. ALTER TABLE is a data definition statement that should be used during system development, not at the application level.

So, an ENUM or SET column should become a separate table whose primary key is a code. Then, the table which refers to this code simply includes it as a foreign key. In the case of SET column, a distinct table would contain the key of the master table plus the key of the table which contains those SET values.

table: sale	column name	sample value
	*internal_number	122
	*date	2006-05-27
	credit_rate_code	F

table: credit_rate	column name	sample value
	*code	F
	description	fixed

Proper validation in the application ensures that the inserted codes belong to the lookup tables.

Multilingual Planning

There is another benefit of using a code table: if we store the car condition new/used, it's more complex to do a multi-lingual application. On the other hand, if we code the car's condition, then we can have a `condition` table and a `language` table:

table: condition	column name	sample value
	language_code	E
	condition_code	N
	description	new

table: language	column name	sample value
	language_code	E
	description	English

Validating the Structure

Validation is done by using precise examples, asking ourselves if we have a column to place all information, covering all cases. Maybe there will be exceptions – what to do with those? Should our structure handle them? We can assess the risk factor associated with those exceptions, versus the cost of handling them and the possible loss in performance for the queries.

An example of an exception: a customer buys two cars the same day – this could influence the choice of primary key, if a date is part of this key, it will be conducive to add a column to this key: the time of day for the sale.

The phpMyAdmin utility can prove useful here. Tables are easily built with this software, while its index management feature permits us to craft our primary keys. Then we can use the multi-table query generator to simulate various reports and what-ifs.

Summary

We have seen that our list of columns needs to be placed into appropriate tables, each having a primary key and respecting some rules for increased efficiency and clarity. We can also improve the model by looking at the scalability and multilingual issues; then we learned a way to validate this model.

5
Data Structure Tuning

This chapter presents various techniques to improve our data structure in terms of security, performance, and documentation. We then present the final data structure for the car dealer's case study.

Data Access Policies

We saw in Chapter 1 that data is an important resource, so access to this resource must be controlled and clearly documented. As each piece of data originates, the responsibility for data entry must be clearly established. After the data has made its way into the database, policies must be in place to control access to it, and these policies are implemented by MySQL's privileges and the use of **views**.

Responsibility

We should determine who in the enterprise – in terms of a person's name or a function name – is responsible for each data element. This should then be documented and a good place to do so is directly in the database structure. An alternative would be to document data responsibility on paper, but information on paper can be easily lost and has a tendency to become obsolete quickly.

In some cases, there will be a primary source and an approbation-level source. Both should be documented – this helps for

- application design, when screens have to reflect the chain of authority for data entry
- privilege management, if direct MySQL data access is granted to end users

phpMyAdmin permits us to describe each column by adding comments to it. If the current MySQL version supports native comments, those will be used; otherwise, phpMyAdmin's linked-tables infrastructure has to be configured to enable the storage

of column comments as meta-data. We will indicate responsibility details for this
column in the corresponding column comment. To reach the page that permits us
to enter comments in phpMyAdmin, we use the left navigation panel to open the
database (here marc) then the table (here car_event). We then click on **Structure** and
choose to edit a field's structure (here event_code) by clicking on the pencil icon.

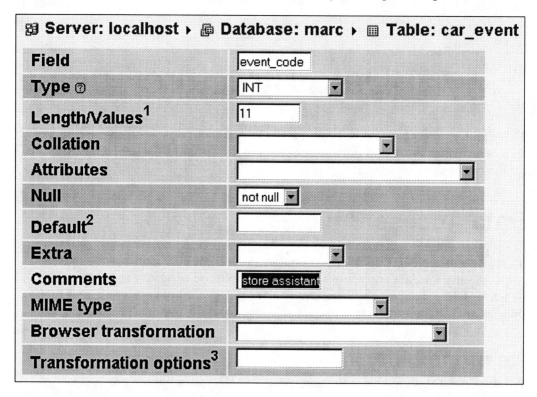

We can then use phpMyAdmin's **Print View** from the **Structure** page to obtain a
listing of the table with comments.

car_event

Field	Type	Null	Default	Links to	Comments
internal_number	int(11)	No			Resp.: Office clerk
moment	datetime	No			Resp.: store assistant
event_code	int(11)	No		event -> code	Resp.: store assistant

Security and Privileges

There are two ways of considering the security of our data. The first and most commonly implemented is at the application level. Normally, applications should ask for credentials: user name, password, and use these credentials to generate web pages or desktop screens that reflect the tasks permitted to this user. Note that the underlying application still connects to MySQL with all the privileges of a developer account but, of course, only shows appropriate data according to the user's rights.

Another issue to consider is when a user has direct access to MySQL, either using a command-line utility or an interface like phpMyAdmin. This might be the case because the end-user application has been developed only to a certain point and does not permit maintenance of code tables, for example. In this case, special MySQL users should be created that have only the needed rights. MySQL supports an access matrix based on rights on databases, tables, columns, and views. This way, we could hide specific columns, like the selling price, to all unauthorized persons.

Views

Since MySQL 5.0, we can build views, which look like tables but are based on queries. These views can be used to:

- hide some columns
- generate modified information based on table columns and the use of expressions on them
- procure a shortcut for data access by joining many tables so as to make them appear as a single table

Since we can associate privileges to these views without giving access to the underlying tables, views can prove handy to let users directly access MySQL and control their actions at the same time.

Here is an example of a view showing the car events and their description – here, we want to hide the event_code column:

```
create view explained_events as
select car_event.internal_number, car_event.moment, event.description
from car_event
left join event on car_event.event_code = event.code
```

Browsing this view in phpMyAdmin displays the following report:

←—T—→	internal_number Resp.:Office clerk	moment Resp.: store assistant	description
□ ✎ ✗	412	2006-05-20 09:58:38	arrived
□ ✎ ✗	500	2006-05-29 16:37:46	washed
□ ✎ ✗	600	2006-05-30 16:38:51	arrived
□ ✎ ✗	700	2006-05-31 16:39:21	arrived

Asking a user to work with views does not mean that this user can only read this data. In many cases, views can be updated. For example, this statement is allowed:

```
UPDATE `explained_events`
SET `moment` = '2006-05-27 09:58:38'
WHERE `explained_events`.`internal_number` = 412;
```

Storage Engines

MySQL is internally structured in such a way that the low-level tasks of storing and managing data are implemented by the **plugable storage engine architecture.** MySQL AB and other companies are active in R&D to improve the offer in the storage engines spectrum. For more information about the architecture itself, refer to http://dev.mysql.com/tech-resources/articles/mysql_5.0_psea1.html.

Every time we create a table, even if we don't notice it, we are asking the MySQL server (implicitly or explicitly) to use one of the available storage engines to store our data physically.

The default and traditional storage engine is named MyISAM. A whole chapter in the *MySQL Reference Manual* (http://dev.mysql.com/doc/refman/5.0/en/storage-engines.html) describes the available engines. Our choice of storage engine can vary from table to table. There is no such thing as a perfect storage engine; we have to choose the best one according to our needs. Here are some points to consider when making a choice:

- MyISAM supports FULLTEXT indexes and compressed read-only storage, and uses about three times less disk space than InnoDB for the equivalent amount of data
- InnoDB offers foreign key constraints, multi-statement transactions with ROLLBACK support; also, due to its locking mechanism, it supports more concurrent SELECT queries than MyISAM
- MEMORY is of course very fast but the content (data) is not permanently stored on-disk, while the table definition itself is on-disk

- NDB (Network DataBase), also called `MySQL Cluster`, offers synchronous replication between the servers – the recommended minimum number of servers in the cluster is four; thus there is no single point of failure in such a cluster

In short, here is a general guideline: if the application requires multi-statement transactions and foreign-key constraints, we should choose `InnoDB`; otherwise, `MyISAM`, the default storage engine, is suggested.

Foreign Key Constraints

The `InnoDB` storage engine (`http://www.innodb.com`), which is included in MySQL offers a facility to describe foreign keys in the table's structure. A **foreign key** is a column (or group of columns) that points to a key in a table. Usually, the key that is pointed to is located in another table and is a primary key of that other table. Foreign keys are commonly used as lookup tables. There are a number of benefits to describing these relations directly in the structure:

- referential integrity of the tables is maintained by the engine – we cannot add an event code into the `car_event` table if the corresponding code is not already present in the `event` table, and we cannot remove a code from the `event` table if it's still referenced by a row in the `car_event` table

- we can program actions that MySQL will accomplish in reaction to certain events; for example, what happens in the referencing table if the referenced code is updated

Let's transpose our `car_event` example into `InnoDB`. Let's first create and populate the referenced table, `event` – notice the `ENGINE=InnoDB` clause:

```
CREATE TABLE `event` (
  `code` int(11) NOT NULL,
  `description` char(40) NOT NULL,
  PRIMARY KEY  (`code`)
) ENGINE=InnoDB DEFAULT CHARSET=latin1;

INSERT INTO `event` VALUES (1, 'washed');
INSERT INTO `event` VALUES (2, 'arrived');
```

Next, the referencing table, `car_event`:

```
CREATE TABLE `car_event` (
  `internal_number` int(11) NOT NULL COMMENT 'Resp.:Office clerk',
  `moment` datetime NOT NULL COMMENT 'Resp.: store assistant',
  `event_code` int(11) NOT NULL COMMENT 'Resp.: store assistant',
  PRIMARY KEY  (`internal_number`),
```

```
      KEY `event_code` (`event_code`)
) ENGINE=InnoDB DEFAULT CHARSET=latin1;

INSERT INTO `car_event` VALUES (412, '2006-05-27 09:58:38', 2);
INSERT INTO `car_event` VALUES (500, '2006-05-29 16:37:46', 1);
INSERT INTO `car_event` VALUES (600, '2006-05-30 16:38:51', 2);
INSERT INTO `car_event` VALUES (700, '2006-05-31 16:39:21', 2);
```

We must have an index on the event_code column to be able to use it in an InnoDB
foreign key constraint, which is defined here:

```
ALTER TABLE `car_event`
  ADD CONSTRAINT `car_event_ibfk_1` FOREIGN KEY (`event_code`)
REFERENCES `event` (`code`) ON UPDATE CASCADE;
```

 The foreign key in car_event can also be defined in the
initial CREATE TABLE statement. The previous example
was done using ALTER TABLE to show that foreign keys
can be added later.

All these operations can be handled in a more visual way via phpMyAdmin. The
Operations sub-page enables us to switch the engine to **InnoDB**:

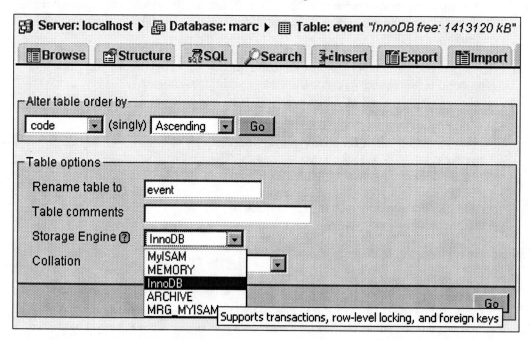

Also, when the tables are under the `InnoDB` storage engine, phpMyAdmin's **Relation view** enables us to define and modify the foreign key and related actions:

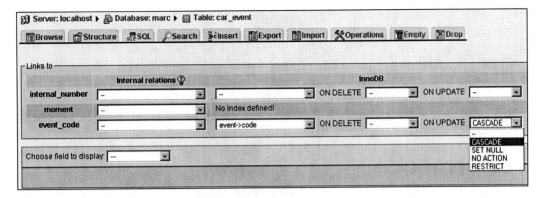

Having defined this ON UPDATE CASCADE clause, let's see what happens when we modify a code value in the `event` table. We decide that the code for **washed** should be **10** instead of **1**:

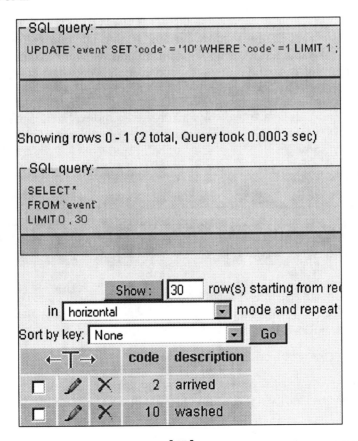

We now browse the `car_event` table; sure enough, the code for **washed** has been changed automatically to the value 10:

←T→	internal_number Resp.:Office clerk	moment Resp.:store assistant	event_code Resp.:store assistant
☐ ✐ ✕	412	2006-05-27 09:58:38	2
☐ ✐ ✕	500	2006-05-29 16:37:46	10
☐ ✐ ✕	600	2006-05-30 16:38:51	washed
☐ ✐ ✕	700	2006-05-31 16:39:21	2

Performance

A number of points must be examined if we want to improve our structure's efficiency in terms of access speed or disk space used.

Indexes

Adding indexes on columns that are used in a WHERE clause is a common way of speeding up the queries. Let's say that we intend to find all vehicles for a specific brand. The `vehicle` table has a `brand_id` column and we want to create an index on this column. In this case, the index won't be unique because each brand is represented by many vehicles.

Using phpMyAdmin, there are two ways to create an index. First, if the index applies to a single column, we can open the **Structure** page for a table and click the index (flash) icon on the same line as the `brand_id` column:

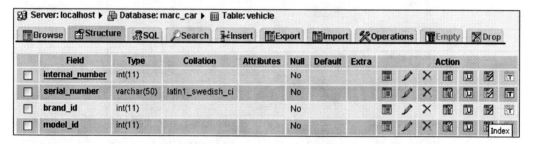

This generates the following statement:

```
ALTER TABLE `vehicle` ADD INDEX(`brand_id`)
```

We could also create an index on a composite key, for example `model_id` plus `year`. For this, we enter the number of columns for our index (two) on the **Structure** page and hit **Go**.

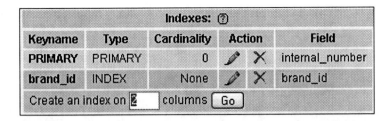

Next, on the index management page, we choose which columns will be part of the index; then we invent a name for this index (here **model-year**) and click **Go** to create it.

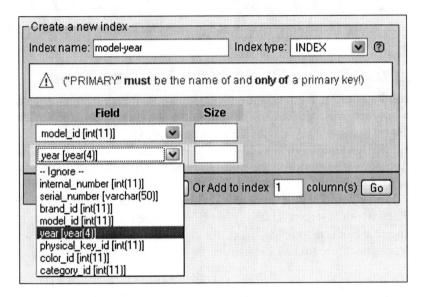

The related SQL command for this action is

```
ALTER TABLE `vehicle` ADD INDEX `model-year` (`model_id`,`year`)
```

To ascertain which index are used on a particular query, we can prefix this query with the EXPLAIN keyword. For example, we issue this command in phpMyAdmin's query box:

```
explain select * from vehicle where brand_id = 1
```

The results tell us that an index on the `brand_id` column is a possible key for retrieval:

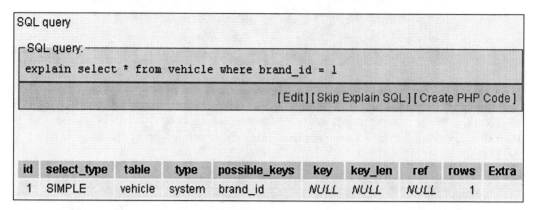

id	select_type	table	type	possible_keys	key	key_len	ref	rows	Extra
1	SIMPLE	vehicle	system	brand_id	*NULL*	*NULL*	*NULL*	1	

Helping the Query Optimizer: Analyze Table

When we send a query to the MySQL server, it uses its query optimizer to find the best way of retrieving the rows. We can help the query optimizer achieve better results by loading a table with data and then executing the ANALYZE TABLE statement on it. This statement asks MySQL to store the key distribution for a table, which means that it counts the number of keys for each index and stores this information for later reuse. For example, after the ANALYZE TABLE on the vehicle table, MySQL might notice that there are 12 different brands, 1000 different vehicles and 100 different model-years. This information will be used later if we ever send a query using one of these indexes. Thus, the ANALYZE TABLE should be executed periodically; the exact frequency depends on the number of updates for this table.

Accessing Replication Slave Servers

MySQL supports a scheme where one-way, asynchronous replication of data occurs between a **master server** and one or more **slave servers**. Since normally, the majority of the requests sent to MySQL are SELECT queries, we can improve response time by sending those read requests to a slave server. This procures a load-balancing effect. Care must be taken to send write-type statements such as INSERT, UPDATE and DELETE to the master.

In current MySQL version (5.0.26), we have to choose the proper server at the application level to achieve this balancing; however, MySQL plans to offer a feature that would automatically send the SELECT queries to slaves.

Replication is an advanced feature of MySQL that should be set up by a seasoned MySQL administrator.

Speed and Data Types

When creating a column, we have to specify a data type for it. Character data types (CHAR, VARCHAR) are very commonly used. For CHAR, we indicate the length of the column (0 to 255), and this column occupies a fixed amount of space. For VARCHAR, each value only takes the space it needs in the table; the indicated length is the maximum length – 255 before MySQL 5.0.3 and 65532 since this version. Numeric types – like INT, FLOAT, and DECIMAL are fixed-length.

To summarize, here are some data types and information about how they are stored:

Data type	Storage method
CHAR	fixed
INT	fixed
FLOAT	fixed
DECIMAL	fixed
VARCHAR	variable

We should be aware that MySQL can silently decide to convert a data type to another one. The reasons for this are explained in the MySQL manual: http://dev.mysql.com/doc/refman/5.0/en/silent-column-changes.html. This is why, after the table's creation, we should re-examine its structure to verify that silent conversion has occurred.

It might seem that we should always choose VARCHAR for character fields, since by using this data type, a shorter value takes less space but there is a reason to still want to use CHAR: speed.

In a table, when all fields are using non-variable data types, the MyISAM storage engine uses a **fixed** table format. In this format, MySQL can predict the size of each row and thus can easily find the distance from, say, one first_name column to the first_name column of the next row. This implies that queries on non-indexed columns are relatively quickly executed. On the contrary, when there is even one VARCHAR column in a table, this is no longer possible, as MyISAM uses **dynamic** table format in this case. Hence, a decision must be made between the speed of data retrieval and the space overhead of using fixed-length columns.

In phpMyAdmin, when looking at a table's structure, the **Row Statistics** section informs us about the fixed or dynamic format:

Row Statistics	
Statements	**Value**
Format	dynamic
Collation	latin1_swedish_ci
Rows	2
Row length ø	28
Row size ø	1,052 Bytes
Creation	May 20, 2006 at 10:56 AM
Last update	May 20, 2006 at 10:56 AM

There is another point in favor of using the fixed format. When rows are deleted, the space previously occupied by these – the holes in the table become available for future insertions so the table does not become physically fragmented.

BLOB and TEXT data types are also variable in length. A BLOB is typically used to store binary data like a car's or a customer's photo. MySQL takes care internally to store these columns separately from the remainder of the table's data, so the impact of having them in a table is not significant.

Table Size Reduction

A utility, myisampack, can be used to transform a MyISAM table into a read-only one while compressing data. In some cases, the table's physical size could be reduced by 70%. This technique is only available if we have access to this command-line utility – there is no SQL query which we can send to achieve this result.

In-Column Data Encoding

The situation I am about to describe happened while I was working on a search engine for bibliographic data but I am transposing it for the car dealer's system.

When we have to migrate data from a pre-existing system into our newly-born data structure, we might encounter data that was formatted in a special way. For example, a list of possible colors for a car model could be expressed as a series of color codes, separated by semi-colons:

```
1A6;1A7;2B7;2T1A65
```

Users of the pre-existing system are comfortable with this method of entering data in this format, and in the case I experienced, users refused to let go of this way of entering data – and they had direct access to the MySQL tables. From a developer's perspective, however, such format makes the task of query generation more complex. Finding the 1A6 color involves splitting the data element, and avoiding the 2T1A65 data element, which also has the 1A6 string.

A proper structure for this case implies getting rid of the semicolon-based format completely and storing just the pure data in table format:

table: model_color	column name	sample value
	*model	1
	color_code	1A6

Another case for which it's even more complex to find coherent data with a query is when there is more than one element between the separators, such as a list of names:

```
Murray Dan; Smith Peter; Black Paul
```

Special care must be taken to avoid matching this list of names when we search for Murray, Paul because Murray and Paul are present in the full string. This case only reinforces the case for moving away from such a format or at least – if we must keep this format due to political issues – for building an intermediary table, which will be used for searching. In this case, the special table must be synchronized whenever the main table's contents changes.

Case Study's Final Structure

In this section we examine the final data structure for our case study. There are many ways to present this structure. First we'll see all the tables that are related to each other – almost all tables are – then we will examine group of related tables and their columns.

The following schema is produced by phpMyAdmin's PDF Page feature. To access this feature, we open a database and access the **Operations** sub-page. Then we click **Edit PDF pages**.

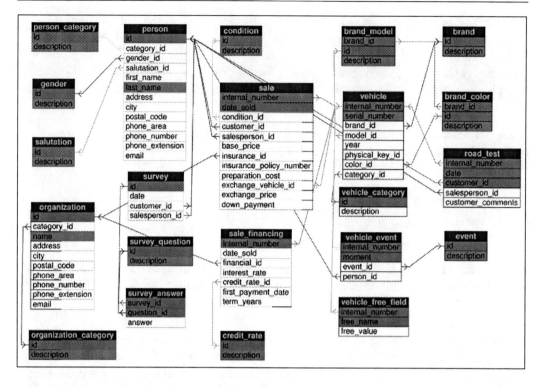

When generating the PDF schema, we can also ask phpMyAdmin to produce a data dictionary. In order to do this, we click the **Data Dictionary** checkbox in the **Display PDF schema** dialog. Here is the page of this dictionary describing the person table:

10 person

Creation: Jun 20, 2006 at 11:14 AM
Last update: Jun 20, 2006 at 11:14 AM

Field	Type	Attributes	Null	Default	Extra	Links to	Comments	MIME
id	int(11)		No					
category_id	int(11)		No			person_category -> id		
gender_id	int(11)		No			gender -> id		
salutation_id	int(11)		No			salutation -> id		
first_name	varchar(50)		No					
last_name	varchar(50)		No					
address	varchar(300)		No					
city	varchar(50)		No					
postal_code	varchar(20)		No					
phone_area	varchar(20)		No					
phone_number	varchar(20)		No					
phone_extension	varchar(20)		No					
email	varchar(100)		No					

This combined data dictionary/schema offers a noteworthy feature: we can click on a table name in the schema to reach the table's description in the dictionary, and the other way around.

The following CREATE TABLE commands come directly from the **Export** feature of phpMyAdmin. To access this feature, simply open a database and choose the **Export** menu, then select all the tables, click the **SQL** checkbox and hit **Go**.

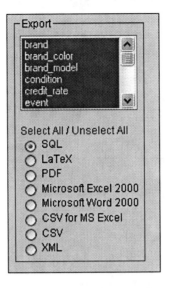

The commands have been grouped into smaller chunks of related tables, even if ultimately there are relations between the tables of those groups. You'll notice that phpMyAdmin adds – in the form of comments in the export file – information about the relations with other tables. Another point to note: the primary key for most tables is id, an integer. Thus, a column pointing to the id column of table brand is named brand_id.

Vehicle

```
--
-- Table structure for table `brand`
--

CREATE TABLE `brand` (
  `id` int(11) NOT NULL,
  `description` varchar(40) NOT NULL,
  PRIMARY KEY  (`id`)
) ENGINE=MyISAM DEFAULT CHARSET=latin1;


-- --------------------------------------------------------
--
-- Table structure for table `brand_color`
--
```

```
CREATE TABLE `brand_color` (
  `brand_id` int(11) NOT NULL,
  `id` int(11) NOT NULL,
  `description` varchar(40) NOT NULL,
  PRIMARY KEY  (`brand_id`,`id`)
) ENGINE=MyISAM DEFAULT CHARSET=latin1;

--
-- RELATIONS FOR TABLE `brand_color`:
--    `brand_id`
--        `brand` -> `id`
--


-- ---------------------------------------------------------
--
-- Table structure for table `brand_model`
--

CREATE TABLE `brand_model` (
  `brand_id` int(11) NOT NULL,
  `id` int(11) NOT NULL,
  `description` varchar(40) NOT NULL,
  PRIMARY KEY  (`brand_id`,`id`)
) ENGINE=MyISAM DEFAULT CHARSET=latin1;

--
-- RELATIONS FOR TABLE `brand_model`:
--    `brand_id`
--        `brand` -> `id`
--


-- ---------------------------------------------------------
--
-- Table structure for table `event`
--

CREATE TABLE `event` (
  `id` int(11) NOT NULL,
  `description` varchar(40) NOT NULL,
  PRIMARY KEY  (`id`)
) ENGINE=MyISAM DEFAULT CHARSET=latin1;

-- ---------------------------------------------------------
--
-- Table structure for table `vehicle`
--
```

```
CREATE TABLE `vehicle` (
  `internal_number` int(11) NOT NULL,
  `serial_number` varchar(50) NOT NULL,
  `brand_id` int(11) NOT NULL,
  `model_id` int(11) NOT NULL,
  `year` year(4) NOT NULL,
  `physical_key_id` int(11) NOT NULL,
  `color_id` int(11) NOT NULL,
  `category_id` int(11) NOT NULL,
  PRIMARY KEY  (`internal_number`)
) ENGINE=MyISAM DEFAULT CHARSET=latin1;

--
-- RELATIONS FOR TABLE `vehicle`:
--    `brand_id`
--        `brand` -> `id`
--    `category_id`
--        `vehicle_category` -> `id`
--    `color_id`
--        `brand_color` -> `id`
--    `model_id`
--        `brand_model` -> `id`
--
-- ------------------------------------------------------------
--
-- Table structure for table `vehicle_category`
--

CREATE TABLE `vehicle_category` (
  `id` int(11) NOT NULL,
  `description` varchar(40) NOT NULL,
  PRIMARY KEY  (`id`)
) ENGINE=MyISAM DEFAULT CHARSET=latin1;

-- ------------------------------------------------------------
--
-- Table structure for table `vehicle_event`
--

CREATE TABLE `vehicle_event` (
  `internal_number` int(11) NOT NULL,
  `moment` date NOT NULL,
  `event_id` int(11) NOT NULL,
  `person_id` int(11) NOT NULL,
  PRIMARY KEY  (`internal_number`,`moment`)
```

```
) ENGINE=MyISAM DEFAULT CHARSET=latin1;

--
-- RELATIONS FOR TABLE `vehicle_event`:
--    `event_id`
--         `event` -> `id`
--    `internal_number`
--         `vehicle` -> `internal_number`
--    `person_id`
--         `person` -> `id`
--
```

Person

```
--
-- Table structure for table `gender`
--

CREATE TABLE `gender` (
  `id` TINYINT(4) NOT NULL,
  `description` varchar(40) NOT NULL,
  PRIMARY KEY  (`id`)
) ENGINE=MyISAM DEFAULT CHARSET=latin1;

-- ------------------------------------------------------------
--
-- Table structure for table `person`
--

CREATE TABLE `person` (
  `id` int(11) NOT NULL,
  `category_id` int(11) NOT NULL,
  `gender_id` TINYINT(4) NOT NULL,
  `salutation_id` TINYINT(4) NOT NULL,
  `first_name` varchar(50) NOT NULL,
  `last_name` varchar(50) NOT NULL,
  `address` varchar(300) NOT NULL,
  `city` varchar(50) NOT NULL,
  `postal_code` varchar(20) NOT NULL,
  `phone_area` varchar(20) NOT NULL,
  `phone_number` varchar(20) NOT NULL,
  `phone_extension` varchar(20) NOT NULL,
  `email` varchar(100) NOT NULL,
  PRIMARY KEY  (`id`)
) ENGINE=MyISAM DEFAULT CHARSET=latin1;
```

```
--
-- RELATIONS FOR TABLE `person`:
--    `category_id`
--         `person_category` -> `id`
--    `gender_id`
--         `gender` -> `id`
--    `salutation_id`
--         `salutation` -> `id`
--
-- ------------------------------------------------------------
--
-- Table structure for table `person_category`
--

CREATE TABLE `person_category` (
  `id` int(11) NOT NULL,
  `description` varchar(40) NOT NULL,
  PRIMARY KEY  (`id`)
) ENGINE=MyISAM DEFAULT CHARSET=latin1;


-- ------------------------------------------------------------
--
-- Table structure for table `salutation`
--

CREATE TABLE `salutation` (
  `id` TINYINT(4) NOT NULL,
  `description` varchar(40) NOT NULL,
  PRIMARY KEY  (`id`)
) ENGINE=MyISAM DEFAULT CHARSET=latin1;


-- ------------------------------------------------------------
```

Sale

```
--
-- Table structure for table `condition`
--

CREATE TABLE `condition` (
  `id` int(11) NOT NULL,
  `description` char(15) NOT NULL,
  PRIMARY KEY  (`id`)
) ENGINE=MyISAM DEFAULT CHARSET=latin1;
-- ------------------------------------------------------------
```

```
--
-- Table structure for table `credit_rate`
--

CREATE TABLE `credit_rate` (
  `id` int(11) NOT NULL,
  `description` char(30) NOT NULL,
  PRIMARY KEY  (`id`)
) ENGINE=MyISAM DEFAULT CHARSET=latin1;


-- ------------------------------------------------------------
--
-- Table structure for table `sale`
--

CREATE TABLE `sale` (
  `internal_number` int(11) NOT NULL,
  `date_sold` date NOT NULL,
  `condition_id` int(11) NOT NULL,
  `customer_id` int(11) NOT NULL,
  `salesperson_id` int(11) NOT NULL,
  `base_price` decimal(9,2) NOT NULL,
  `insurance_id` int(11) NOT NULL,
  `insurance_policy_number` varchar(40) NOT NULL,
  `preparation_cost` decimal(9,2) NOT NULL,
  `exchange_vehicle_id` int(11) NOT NULL,
  `exchange_price` decimal(9,2) NOT NULL,
  `down_payment` decimal(9,2) NOT NULL,
  PRIMARY KEY  (`internal_number`,`date_sold`)
) ENGINE=MyISAM DEFAULT CHARSET=latin1;

--
-- RELATIONS FOR TABLE `sale`:
--   `condition_id`
--       `condition` -> `id`
--   `customer_id`
--       `person` -> `id`
--   `exchange_vehicle_id`
--       `vehicle` -> `internal_number`
--   `insurance_id`
--       `organization` -> `id`
--   `internal_number`
--       `vehicle` -> `internal_number`
--   `salesperson_id`
--       `person` -> `id`
```

```
--
-- ------------------------------------------------------
--
-- Table structure for table `sale_financing`
--

CREATE TABLE `sale_financing` (
  `internal_number` int(11) NOT NULL auto_increment,
  `date_sold` date NOT NULL,
  `financial_id` int(11) NOT NULL,
  `interest_rate` decimal(9,4) NOT NULL,
  `credit_rate_id` int(11) NOT NULL,
  `first_payment_date` date NOT NULL,
  `term_years` int(11) NOT NULL,
  PRIMARY KEY  (`internal_number`)
) ENGINE=MyISAM DEFAULT CHARSET=latin1 AUTO_INCREMENT=1 ;


--
-- RELATIONS FOR TABLE `sale_financing`:
--    `credit_rate_id`
--        `credit_rate` -> `id`
--    `financial_id`
--        `organization` -> `id`
--    `internal_number`
--        `vehicle` -> `internal_number`
--


-- ------------------------------------------------------
--
-- Table structure for table `tax_rate`
--

CREATE TABLE `tax_rate` (
  `start_date` date NOT NULL,
  `end_date` date NOT NULL,
  `rate` decimal(9,4) NOT NULL,
  PRIMARY KEY  (`start_date`,`end_date`)
) ENGINE=MyISAM DEFAULT CHARSET=latin1;


-- ------------------------------------------------------
```

Other tables

```
--
-- Table structure for table `parameters`
--

CREATE TABLE `parameters` (
  `dealer_number` varchar(30) NOT NULL
) ENGINE=MyISAM DEFAULT CHARSET=latin1;


-- ------------------------------------------------------------
--
-- Table structure for table `organization`
--

CREATE TABLE `organization` (
  `id` int(11) NOT NULL,
  `category_id` int(11) NOT NULL,
  `name` varchar(50) NOT NULL,
  `address` varchar(300) NOT NULL,
  `city` varchar(50) NOT NULL,
  `postal_code` varchar(20) NOT NULL,
  `phone_area` varchar(20) NOT NULL,
  `phone_number` varchar(20) NOT NULL,
  `phone_extension` varchar(20) NOT NULL,
  `email` varchar(100) NOT NULL,
  PRIMARY KEY  (`id`)
) ENGINE=MyISAM DEFAULT CHARSET=latin1;

--
-- RELATIONS FOR TABLE `organization`:
--    `category_id`
--        `organization_category` -> `id`
--


-- ------------------------------------------------------------
--
-- Table structure for table `organization_category`
--

CREATE TABLE `organization_category` (
  `id` int(11) NOT NULL,
  `description` varchar(40) NOT NULL,
  PRIMARY KEY  (`id`)
) ENGINE=MyISAM DEFAULT CHARSET=latin1;
-- ------------------------------------------------------------
```

```
--
-- Table structure for table `road_test`
--

CREATE TABLE `road_test` (
  `internal_number` int(11) NOT NULL,
  `date` date NOT NULL,
  `customer_id` int(11) NOT NULL,
  `salesperson_id` int(11) NOT NULL,
  `customer_comments` varchar(255) NOT NULL,
  PRIMARY KEY  (`internal_number`,`date`,`customer_id`)
) ENGINE=MyISAM DEFAULT CHARSET=latin1;


--
-- RELATIONS FOR TABLE `road_test`:
--    `customer_id`
--        `person` -> `id`
--    `internal_number`
--        `vehicle` -> `internal_number`
--    `salesperson_id`
--        `person` -> `id`
--


-- ---------------------------------------------------------
--
-- Table structure for table `survey`
--

CREATE TABLE `survey` (
  `id` int(11) NOT NULL,
  `date` date NOT NULL,
  `customer_id` int(11) NOT NULL,
  `salesperson_id` int(11) NOT NULL,
  PRIMARY KEY  (`id`)
) ENGINE=MyISAM DEFAULT CHARSET=latin1;


--
-- RELATIONS FOR TABLE `survey`:
--    `customer_id`
--        `person` -> `id`
--    `salesperson_id`
--        `person` -> `id`
--


-- ---------------------------------------------------------
--
```

```
-- Table structure for table `survey_answer`
--

CREATE TABLE `survey_answer` (
  `survey_id` int(11) NOT NULL,
  `question_id` int(11) NOT NULL,
  `answer` varchar(30) NOT NULL,
  PRIMARY KEY  (`survey_id`,`question_id`)
) ENGINE=MyISAM DEFAULT CHARSET=latin1;


--
-- RELATIONS FOR TABLE `survey_answer`:
--    `question_id`
--        `survey_question` -> `id`
--    `survey_id`
--        `survey` -> `id`
--


-- ----------------------------------------------------------
--
-- Table structure for table `survey_question`
--

CREATE TABLE `survey_question` (
  `id` int(11) NOT NULL,
  `description` varchar(40) NOT NULL,
  PRIMARY KEY  (`id`)
) ENGINE=MyISAM DEFAULT CHARSET=latin1;
-- ----------------------------------------------------------
```

Summary

We improved our data structure's implementation by assessing the responsible person for each data element and by storing this information into column comments. We then saw how to use privileges and views to improve security, how to choose the best storage engine per table, and how to benefit from foreign key constraints. Performance issues were considered, and then we were presented with the final model for the car dealer's case study.

6

Supplemental Case Study

Now, it's time to apply our newly learned principles to a completely different theme. We upgrade from cars to planes, covering a simple airline system.

This chapter's case study does not pretend to encompass the full collection of data from real airline – it's only a sample. Nonetheless, we'll see that the principles we learned previously can be applied to build and refine a correct and coherent data structure.

Normally, each airline has its own information system. We assume here that we have got the mandate to build an information system that encompasses many airlines.

Results from the Document Gathering Phase

After reviewing the airline system's current website, a booking agent's website, some electronic tickets, and boarding passes, we gather a large amount of information. We'll first express this information with sentences which present the system and data exchange on a rather high level. Each sentence is followed by a list of the data elements which we can deduce from it. An element can be present in more than one sentence. Refer to the *Tables and Sample Values* section for more details about each data element. There are also some notes that will help us in the naming and grouping phase.

Flight 456 of Air Quebec leaves Montreal-Trudeau airport at 22:45 on October 2nd, 2007 heading for Paris's Charles de Gaulle.

The following are the data elements that can be obtained from the above sentence:

- flight_number
- airline_name

- airport_name
- flight_departure_moment

We need to indicate whether the airport is for departure or arrival.

The airport code for Montreal-Trudeau is YUL and the one for Charles de Gaulle is CDG.

The data element obtained from the above sentence is:

- airport_code

Should we use the airport_code as a primary key? Maybe not, due to space considerations.

This flight is scheduled to land at 11:30 the day after (local time).

The data element obtained is:

- flight_arrival_moment

Do we need to split the date and time into two fields? Probably not, to benefit from date and time calculations functions (how many hours and minutes takes a flight, taking the date into account).

An aircraft model APM-300 from Fontax services this flight.

The data elements obtained from above sentence are:

- plane_model
- plane_brand

Do we need to associate the plane model to a flight, but also to which specific plane. (There can be more than one APM-300.)

The pilot on this flight is Dan Murray and the flight attendant is Melanie Waters. Other crew members are to be confirmed.

The data elements obtained from the above sentence are:

- pilot_first_name
- pilot_last_name
- flight_attendant_first_name
- flight_attendant_last_name

We should generalize using the notion of a crew category.

Peter Smith buys a ticket for this flight from Fantastic Tour, Inc., a booking agency. The ticket number is 014 88417654. This is a one-way ticket.

The data elements obtained from the above sentence are:

- passenger_first_name
- passenger_last_name
- booking_agency_name
- ticket_number
- ticket_type

We'll also need a primary key for the passenger and probably for the booking agency if we don't use its code. Should the ticket itself be represented in a table, or will the ticket number be part of something more general like a reservation?

For this flight, Mr. Smith is seated at 19A, located in the economy section of the plane.

The data elements obtained from the above sentence are:

- passenger_last_name
- seat_id
- plane_section

The sections available on a plane depend not only on the plane model but also on the airline.

This ticket is non-refundable.

The data element obtained from the above sentence is:

- ticket_refundability

Flight 456 can be boarded at gate number 74, 35 minutes before takeoff.

The data elements obtained from the above sentence are:

- flight_number
- gate_id
- boarding_time

In economy class, passengers are entitled to one bag inside the cabin and two registered bags – total weight 50 kg max. Mr Smith has one registered bag, bearing the tag AQ636-84763.

The data elements obtained from the above sentence are:

- plane_section
- max_number_in_cabin_bags
- max_number_registered_bags
- max_weight_registered_bags_kg
- tag_id

 We have detected that "class" is a synonym for "section".

There are information screens in the airport that indicate the state of each flight: on time, boarding, delayed, or cancelled.

The data element obtained from the above sentence is:

- flight_status

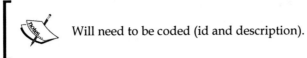

Will need to be coded (id and description).

Two meals are served on this flight. Air Quebec has arrangements with Montreal Chef Service for the preparation and delivery of food.

The data elements obtained from the above sentence are:

- number_meals
- airline_name
- meal_supplier

Air Quebec owns four Fontax APM-300 aircraft but aircraft #302 (code-named Charlie) is scheduled for repairs in October 2007.

The data elements obtained from the above sentence are:

- airline_name
- plane_brand
- plane_model
- plane_id
- description
- plane_event
- plane_event_start_moment
- plane_event_end_moment

Each plane is affectionately nicknamed, the element for this will be "description". About the repairs, we generalize them with the concept of events, having a starting and ending moment.

Passenger Smith can use the quick reference code A6BCUD and his last name to access his flight information on the airline web site.

The data elements obtained from the above sentence are:

- passenger_last_name
- web_site_quick_reference

Preliminary List of Data Elements

We list here the data elements as they can be deduced from the document gathering phase. In many cases, they are not in a format already suitable for the final model because they are prefixed with a table name. For example, a data element identified as `pilot_last_name` will become the column `last_name` in the `pilot` table. Sample values and more detailed information about each data element appear in the next section.

Data elements	
flight_departure_moment	seat_id
flight_arrival_moment	plane_section
departure_airport_code	ticket_refundability
arrival_airport_code	gate_id
airline_code	boarding_time
airline_name	max_number_in_cabin_bags
airport_name	max_number_registered_bags
plane_brand	max_weight_registered_bags_kg
plane_model	tag_id
pilot_last_name	ticket_issued_on
pilot_first_name	number_meals
flight_attendant_last_name	web_site_quick_reference
flight_attendant_first_name	meal_supplier
passenger_last_name	plane_id
passenger_first_name	plane_event
passenger_id	plane_event_start_moment
booking_agency_name	plane_event_end_moment
ticket_number	flight_status

Tables and Sample Values

To prepare the list of tables, we start with the physical objects or persons we can observe in the sentences built from the documents gathering phase. Then we have a look at all the elements and build new tables to accommodate them.

In the following table descriptions, the table layout is followed by design comments when appropriate.

Code Tables

Usually the following tables are designed first because they are easier to model and they are needed for establishing the relations from more complex tables.

table: airport	column name	sample value
	*id	1
	international_code	YUL
	description	Montreal-Trudeau

The airport table could contain other columns like the address, phone, and website.

table: airline	column name	sample value
	*id	1
	description	Air-Quebec

table: plane_brand	column name	sample value
	*id	1
	description	Fontax

We avoid naming this table as brand because it's a too generic name.

table: meal_supplier	column name	sample value
	*id	9
	description	Montreal Chef Service

table: booking_agency	column name	sample value
	*id	1
	description	Fantastic Tour

Again, this table could have more details about the agency, like phone and address. We could also merge this table with meal_supplier table by adding a code identifying the type of company, but it's not done in the present model.

table: ticket_type	column name	sample value
	*id	1
	description	one-way

table: crew_category	column name	sample value
	*id	1
	description	Pilot

To avoid columns like `pilot_last_name`, `copilot_first_name`, we form a `crew_category` table. See also the related `flight_crew` table later in this chapter.

table: ticket_refundability	column name	sample value
	*id	1
	description	non-refundable

table: flight_status	column name	sample value
	*id	1
	description	boarding

table: event	column name	sample value
	*id	1
	description	repair

If we need to include other types of events in the model, this `event` table will have to be renamed as something more precise like `plane_event`, and a new name will be needed for our current `plane_event` table that is used to associate an event with a plane.

Themed Tables

These tables are more comprehensive than the code tables. Each one refers to a specific theme that needs more columns than a simple code table.

table: plane	column name	sample value
	*id	302
	airline_id	1
	brand_id	1
	model_id	2
	description	Charlie

This table identifies which aircraft belongs to which airline, with the description being an internal means of describing this particular aircraft within the airline. Other fields like an aircraft serial number can be added here.

table: passenger	column name	sample value
	*id	1302
	last_name	Smith
	first_name	Peter
	passport_info	CDN234234

table: crew	column name	sample value
	*id	9
	category_id	1
	last_name	Murray
	first_name	Dan

Passengers and crew members cannot be physically merged into one table even if they belong to the same flight because the set of columns used to describe a passenger diverges from the one associated to a crew member. We'll cover in the *Sample Queries* section how to produce a combined list of all persons on a plane.

table: flight	column name	sample value
	*id	34
	airline_id	1
	number	456
	departure_moment	2007-10-02 22:45
	arrival_moment	2007-10-03 11:30
	departure_airport_id	1
	arrival_airport_id	2
	plane_id	302
	meal_supplier_id	9
	number_meals	2
	departure_gate	74
	arrival_gate	B65
	boarding_moment	2007-10-02 22:10
	status_id	1

The notion of flight is central to this system, thus we'll have a `flight` table. This means that we have to determine a primary key and, at first sight, the flight number would be a good candidate – but it's not and the reason for this is that the flight number is not painted on an aircraft; it's only a logical way of expressing the movement of a plane between two airports, and also the persons or companies related to this movement. We note that the flight number is kept short – three or four digits for improved reference on all printed matter and on airport information screens; thus, this flight number is only meaningful when accompanied by supplemental information, like the airline code (AQ) or company name, and a date.

Keeping in mind that there will be other tables associated with this flight table, we have two choices here for the primary key:

- create a **surrogate key** (an artificial primary key whose value is not derived from other table's data)

- use a combination of columns – airline_id, flight_number, departure_moment

It is better to create a surrogate key, id. This id will be propagated to the related tables in just one column, which could help to speed up retrieval times because there is just one field to compare between tables. Using the flight's id will also simplify the writing of queries. Of course we include the flight number – the information known to the public in the `flight` table but not as a primary key.

table: reservation	column name	sample value
	*flight_id	34
	*passenger_id	1302
	web_site_quick_reference	KARTYU
	ticket_number	014 88417654
	ticket_issued_moment	2007-01-01 12:00
	booking_agency_id	1
	ticket_refundability_id	1
	ticket_type_id	1
	seat	19A
	section_id	2

It would be a mistake to include columns such as `passenger1`, `passenger2` or `seat_1a`, `seat_1b` in the flights table. This is why we use the `reservation` table to hold passenger information related to a specific flight. This table could also be named `flight_passenger`.

Normally we would not need the section_id in the reservation table, since we can refer to it via the seat_id but the seat_id may be unknown at the time of reservation, so seat assignment can be delayed until the boarding pass is issued.

Composite-Key Tables

These tables have more than one key because some key segments refer to a code or themed table.

table: plane_brand_ model	column name	sample value
	*brand_id	1
	*id	2
	description	APM-300

Here, the brand_id and a unique id form the primary keys for the plane model. We want to know to which brand this model refers, and still keep integers for the keys instead of using APM-300 as a key value.

table: plane_section	column name	sample value
	*airline_id	1
	*id	1
	description	economy

Each airline can potentially describe the sections of their planes the way they want – some are using *hospitality* instead of *economy*.

table: airline_brand_model_ restriction	column name	sample value
	*airline_id	1
	*brand_id	1
	*model_id	2
	max_number_in_cabin_bags	1
	max_number_registered_bags	2
	max_weight_registered_bags_kg	50

table: plane_section_seat	column name	sample value
	*airline_id	1
	*brand_id	1
	*model_id	2
	*section_id	1
	*seat	19A

The `plane_section_seat` table describes which seats are located in a specific section of the aircraft. This is per airline, brand, model, and section, because different airlines could possess the same kind of aircraft but use different seat numbers or have a larger business section than others airlines. Also, in some cases, seats 1A and 1C may exist but 1B may not. Thus, we need this table to hold the complete list of existing seats.

table:flight_crew	column name	sample value
	*flight_id	34
	*crew_id	9

With these sample values, we can deduce that Dan Murray is the pilot for flight 456 of Air-Quebec. Another possible column in this table would be the status of this crew member for this flight: arrived on time, cancelled, or replaced.

table: plane_event	column name	sample value
	*plane_id	302
	*event_id	1
	*start_moment	2008-10-01
	end_moment	2008-10-31

table: reservation_registered_ bags	column name	sample value
	*flight_id	34
	*passenger_id	1302
	*tag	AQ636-84763

Other columns for tag tracking could be added here.

Airline System Data Schema

Here again we use phpMyAdmin's PDF schema feature to display the relations between tables and the keys involved.

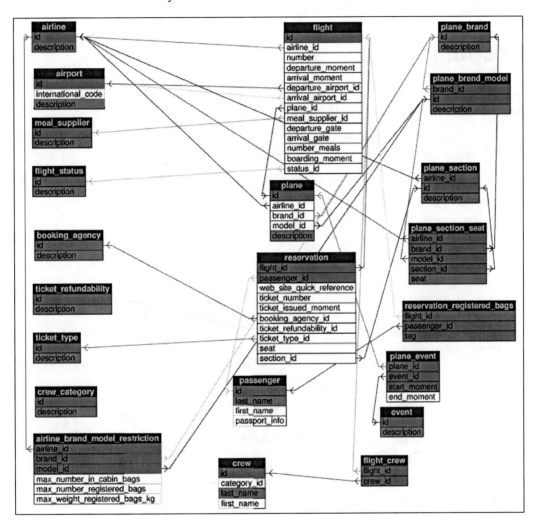

Sample Queries

As a complement to the list of tables and the database schema, let's see our tables in action! We will enter sample values into the tables, and then build some SQL queries in order to pull the needed data.

Inserting Sample Values

We use the sample values described in the above list of tables. Please refer to this book's support site (http://www.packtpub.com/support) for the code download which contains the tables' definition and sample values.

Boarding Pass

A passenger can print his or her boarding pass while at home by using the website's quick reference for his or her reservation, which is KARTYU in our example. Here is the generated query to retrieve the boarding pass information:

```
select passenger.last_name,
passenger.first_name,
flight.number,
airline.description,
flight.departure_moment,
flight.departure_gate,
flight.boarding_moment,
reservation.seat,
plane_section.description
from reservation
inner join passenger on reservation.passenger_id = passenger.id
inner join flight on reservation.flight_id = flight.id
inner join airline on flight.airline_id = airline.id
inner join plane_section on (airline.id = plane_section.airline_id
                    and reservation.section_id = plane_section.id)
where reservation.web_site_quick_reference = 'KARTYU'
```

Executing this query retrieves these results:

last_name	first_name	number	description	departure_moment	departure_gate	boarding_moment	seat	description
Smith	Peter	456	Air-Québec	2007-10-02 22:45:00	74	2007-10-02 22:10:00	19A	economy

Passenger List

Here, the airline wants a list of passengers for a specific flight; we use flight_id, which is the primary key of the flight table, and not the flight number because flight numbers are not unique.

```
select
reservation.seat,
passenger.last_name,
passenger.first_name,
```

```
passenger.passport_info,
airline.description,
flight.number
from reservation
inner join passenger on reservation.passenger_id = passenger.id
inner join flight on reservation.flight_id = flight.id
inner join airline on flight.airline_id = airline.id
where reservation.flight_id = 34
order by reservation.seat
```

Currently, this flight is not very popular, and it looks like Peter and Annie will be able to chat together:

seat	last_name	first_name	passport_info	description	number
19A	Smith	Peter	CDN234234	Air-Québec	456
19B	Delisle	Annie	CDN123456	Air-Québec	456

All Persons on a Flight

In the unlikely event of a plane crash, we might need to extract quickly the list of all persons on a flight. The following query does just that:

```
select
passenger.last_name as 'last name',
passenger.first_name as 'first name',
'passenger' as 'type',
airline.description,
flight.number
from reservation
inner join passenger on reservation.passenger_id = passenger.id
inner join flight on reservation.flight_id = flight.id
inner join airline on flight.airline_id = airline.id
where reservation.flight_id = 34
union
select
crew.last_name as 'last name',
crew.first_name as 'first name',
'crew' as 'type',
airline.description,
flight.number
from flight_crew
inner join crew on flight_crew.crew_id = crew.id
inner join flight on flight_crew.flight_id = flight.id
inner join airline on flight.airline_id = airline.id
```

```
where flight_crew.flight_id = 34
order by 'last name', 'first name'
```

The results are sorted by last name and first name; note the "type" column that indicates whether this person is a passenger or a crew member.

last name	first name	type	description	number
Delisle	Annie	passenger	Air-Québec	456
Murray	Dan	crew	Air-Québec	456
Smith	Peter	passenger	Air-Québec	456

Summary

From the study of a few documents about an airline system, we listed the possible data elements that become columns grouped into tables. We carefully chose the primary key or keys for each table and built relations between these tables, verifying that all potential data elements were included in at least one table.

Index

**Thank you for buying
Creating your MySQL Database:
Practical Design Tips and Techniques**

Packt Open Source Project Royalties

When we sell a book written on an Open Source project, we pay a royalty directly to that project. Therefore by purchasing Creating your MySQL Database: Practical Design Tips and Techniques, Packt will have given some of the money received to the MySQL project.

In the long term, we see ourselves and you—customers and readers of our books—as part of the Open Source ecosystem, providing sustainable revenue for the projects we publish on. Our aim at Packt is to establish publishing royalties as an essential part of the service and support a business model that sustains Open Source.

If you're working with an Open Source project that you would like us to publish on, and subsequently pay royalties to, please get in touch with us.

Writing for Packt

We welcome all inquiries from people who are interested in authoring. Book proposals should be sent to authors@packtpub.com. If your book idea is still at an early stage and you would like to discuss it first before writing a formal book proposal, contact us; one of our commissioning editors will get in touch with you.

We're not just looking for published authors; if you have strong technical skills but no writing experience, our experienced editors can help you develop a writing career, or simply get some additional reward for your expertise.

About Packt Publishing

Packt, pronounced 'packed', published its first book "Mastering phpMyAdmin for Effective MySQL Management" in April 2004 and subsequently continued to specialize in publishing highly focused books on specific technologies and solutions.

Our books and publications share the experiences of your fellow IT professionals in adapting and customizing today's systems, applications, and frameworks. Our solution-based books give you the knowledge and power to customize the software and technologies you're using to get the job done. Packt books are more specific and less general than the IT books you have seen in the past. Our unique business model allows us to bring you more focused information, giving you more of what you need to know, and less of what you don't.

Packt is a modern, yet unique publishing company, which focuses on producing quality, cutting-edge books for communities of developers, administrators, and newbies alike. For more information, please visit our website: www.PacktPub.com.

Mastering phpMyAdmin 2.8 for Effective MySQL Management

ISBN: 1-847191-60-6   Paperback: 248 pages

Increase your MySQL productivity and control by discovering the real power of phpMyAdmin 2.8

1. Effectively administrate your MySQL databases

2. Manage users and privileges with MySQL Server Administration tools

3. Get to grips with the hidden features and capabilities of phpMyAdmin

Building Websites with Joomla!

ISBN: 1-904811-94-9   Paperback: 250 pages

A step by step tutorial to getting your Joomla! CMS website up fast

1. Walk through each step in a friendly and accessible way

2. Customize and extend your Joomla! site

3. Get your Joomla! website up fast

Please check **www.PacktPub.com** for information on our titles

Building Websites with XOOPS : A step-by-step tutorial

ISBN: 1-904811-28-0 Paperback: 180 pages

Get your XOOPS website up fast using this easy-to-follow guide

1. Simple and practical guide to XOOPS

2. Manage blocks, modules, users, and themes

3. Case study reinforces effective learning

Smarty PHP Template Programming and Applications

ISBN: 1-904811-40-X Paperback: 250 pages

A step-by-step guide to building PHP websites and applications using the Smarty templating engine

1. Bring the benefits of Smarty to your PHP programming

2. Give your designers the power to modify content and layout without PHP programming

3. Produce code that is easier to debug, maintain, and modify

4. Useful for both Smarty developers and users

Please check **www.PacktPub.com** for information on our titles

Printed in the United States
95146LV00004B/5/A